Like Your Neighbor?

DOING EVERYDAY EVANGELISM
ON COMMON GROUND

Stephen W. Sorenson

≋
InterVarsity Press
Downers Grove, Illinois

InterVarsity Press
P.O. Box 1400, Downers Grove, IL 60515-1426
World Wide Web: www.ivpress.com

InterVarsity Press® *is the book-publishing division of InterVarsity Christian Fellowship/USA*®, *a student movement active on campus at hundreds of universities, colleges and schools of nursing in the United States of America, and a member movement of the International Fellowship of Evangelical Students. For information about local and regional activities, write Public Relations Dept., InterVarsity Christian Fellowship/USA, 6400 Schroeder Rd., P.O. Box 7895, Madison, WI 53707-7895, or visit the IVCF website at <www.intervarsity.org>.*

While all of the stories in this book are true, names and identifying details have often been changed to protect the privacy of the individuals involved.

Design: Cindy Kiple
Images: IVP Images
ISBN 0-8308-3264-5
Printed in the United States of America ∞

To my father, Mel Sorenson,

whose faith and strength inspire me.

Contents

Breaking Down Our Stereotypes

Frankly, I love irreligious people. Some of my best friends are, in reality,

hell-bound pagans, and I am impassioned about wanting to see them transformed by

the same amazing grace that radically redirected the trajectory of my own life.

LEE STROBEL

Robert showed up at our home one morning ready to help us install large windows into the attached garage we were building. I'd never met him before, but he wanted to work for free. Roy, my father-in-law, had described our building project to him during a flight to Colorado a week earlier.

"I'll be in Colorado for a few weeks," Robert had said, "and I'd be glad to help out." So Roy had given him our address.

To say I was pleased that Robert showed up would be a drastic understatement. Both my wrists were in braces from recent tendon injuries, and I was incredibly frustrated at not being able to help with the construction. With Robert's help, we'd have enough manpower to accomplish quite a bit before cold weather and snow arrived.

For a number of days, Robert moved lumber, pounded nails, ran a chainsaw and helped to install windows. I'd seldom seen a harder worker, much less someone who was working for free to help people he barely knew.

Often he and I talked during lunchtime. I discovered that he had been a musician in the military but developed a disease and could no longer listen to or play the music he loved so dearly.

Early one afternoon, I felt strongly that I was supposed to talk with Robert about spiritual things. But I quickly stifled the impulse. *After all, I thought, he is working on a ladder, seems quite content with where he is in life despite the challenges he has faced and is graciously sacrificing many hours to make up for my inability to work. He is also quite well read on subjects I know little about, and I know virtually nothing about his spiritual background. There's no way he will be open to hearing about Jesus.*

But the promptings continued, from a source I later recognized as the Holy Spirit. So I finally stepped out of my comfort zone and said something profound like "Hey Robert, why don't you take a break and come talk with me?"

"I can't," he replied, smiling. "I've got to finish nailing this."

"Sure you can," I pressed. "Half an hour's break won't hurt anything."

Moments later, as we rested beneath pine trees south of the house, I shared a two-minute story about something that God had done for me. To be honest, I was pretty uncomfortable. I didn't want Robert to feel pressured, and I expected him to change the subject immediately.

But that didn't happen. Robert began telling me about his early life, about spiritual things he had been taught and how he had drifted away from God. He revealed the pain he'd felt when he had to give up his music and told me he understood a bit of how I felt not being able to do physical activities I loved. All the reasons I'd had for not approaching him about spiritual things disappeared.

About forty-five minutes later, Robert prayed to receive Jesus—a few days before he continued his travels.

I connected with Robert several years later, again in a somewhat miraculous way. He was traveling through Colorado but didn't remember our last name. But he heard my wife and me being interviewed on the radio. Recognizing our voices, he listened for our last name and called us from a phone booth to get directions to our house! As it turned out, he was still growing as a Christian and had been sharing his faith with others as he traveled.

After literally bringing Robert to our doorstep twice, God seemed to be reinforcing his desire that I become more open to connecting with non-Christians he would bring into my life. I have wondered how Robert's life, and mine, would be different if I hadn't risked sharing a simple gospel message with him that day in the woods and allowed God to handle the rest. I thank God that I listened to his promptings and responded *that time*. (I haven't always listened since then, but I'm learning.)

Years later, a coworker with whom I shared this story asked me, "Would you have talked with him if your wrists weren't injured?"

"No," I replied, "I'd have been working."

"Was all the expense and suffering you had to face in getting your wrists healed worth the opportunity you had, because of those injuries, to share Jesus with Robert?"

Despite the two years of debilitation and rehabilitation, I knew the answer immediately. Yes, from a kingdom perspective it has been worth it. Jesus went to the cross for Robert and for me, and every time a person receives Jesus the angels rejoice! In light of Robert's eternal future in heaven, two years of pain was a small price to pay. That doesn't mean I'd want to experience that suffering again, but I am thankful that I began to grasp more of what the apostle Paul meant when he wrote in Philippians 3:20, "But our citizenship is in heaven."

In this instance, God used my injuries to make me more sensitive to him and to Robert and allowed me to experience the joy of being with Robert when he met Jesus for the first time. I treasure that moment, and I'm humbled to think that God wants to use *me*—with all my shortcomings and doubts and fears—every day.

Much is happening invisibly all around us in the spiritual world, and I'm thankful for times when I get glimpses of the big picture of God's redemptive work on earth. They fill me with joy and make me more eager to be fully yielded to God so I can become like the clay mentioned in Romans 9:20-21. These glimpses also make me aware of the insignificance of many earthly things that I can't take with me when I die. Someday, though, I hope to meet others in heaven with whom Robert shared the message of Jesus.

CHOICES

For years, growing up in fundamentalist churches, I heard Christians say, "We are supposed to be 'in the world and not of the world.'" They interpreted that phrase to mean more "dos and don'ts" that put up walls of separation rather than considering how they could reflect the light of Christ to people in spiritual darkness.

Sadly, I bought into this line of thinking. I recall various times when I worked hard to keep a safe distance from non-Christians or at least to figure out ways to avoid making in-depth connections with them. They intimidated me: I wasn't sure I could answer their questions, and some activities they enjoyed were quite different from mine. I didn't want to take risks. Deep inside, I also faced this haunting question: *What do I really have to offer them? Some of them seem so happy and successful. Others clearly don't want anything to do with God, and if I bring up my Christian faith I might alienate them.*

MEET THE PARENT(S) OF YOUR CHILD'S FRIENDS

My wife and I often met non-Christians while picking up our child from sporting events, school fairs, birthday parties and the like. Building on our children's common activities, we have asked parents questions about their children and themselves. Then, if appropriate, we have invited them to do something with us, bringing their child(ren) of course!

One dad whom I met through my daughter has become a good friend. Although not a professing Christian, he remains open to discussing spiritual things. Not long ago I told him about a place to cut firewood, and he was able to pick up a few loads. To express thankfulness, he dropped off a load at our house.

Many of my Christian friends felt and acted the same way. We didn't talk openly about the invisible walls we erected. We just ended up in a comfortable rut. Instead of naturally sharing Jesus' love and truth with those with whom we interacted in everyday life, we tried to minimize our contact with them. As a result, we became pretty isolated and comfortable within our own subculture.

Not surprisingly, several things happened. Instead of experiencing the spiritual growth and facing the challenges that would have come as we built relationships with people outside the church, my friends and I focused our attention on smaller issues. We spoke insider "Christianese"—theological words we thought we understood but used to set ourselves apart from other people—and seldom invited non-Christians to attend social activities at church or in our homes. We focused more on ourselves than on what God really wanted to do in and through us. We became subtly legalistic and used the walls we'd created to feel good about ourselves and to fence out other people. Instead of being excited about sharing our faith and the dynamic character of God, we lost much of the joy we had had when we first met Jesus and experienced his transforming power.

Little did we know the spiritual and relational price we were paying.

This type of "wall building" has gone on for a long time, and it continues today. Christians can ignore an "alternative-lifestyle" couple below them in the apartment building or fail to reach out to needy people they pass every week on the way to church. It's often easier to eat lunch with a Christian coworker than to sit with and listen to someone who clearly believes in pursuing all kinds of "worldly" pleasures and treasures and views God with disdain.

We also isolate ourselves in more subtle ways, even alienating people who otherwise might be open to knowing more about Jesus. Not long ago, a neighbor angrily told me how sick he is of seeing newspaper advertisements for "Christian babysitters" and "Christian handymen." "What right do they have," he fumed, "to assume they have some kind of moral superiority over the rest of us?" Good point. Although he doesn't identify himself as a Christian, this man's parents were missionaries overseas, and he and his wife have helped me and my family in countless ways for many years.

When I talk with Christians, individually or in groups, about their relationships with people outside the church, I often hear comments such as these:

- "I'd like to get to know non-Christians, but I don't know how."
- "I'd like to reach out to non-Christians, but I work in a Christian organization and do things with Christian friends on weekends."
- "I don't understand non-Christians—their thinking and lifestyle. They make me uncomfortable."
- "It's easier to be with Christians; we have more in common."
- "I just don't have time to get involved with *them*."

Perhaps you have heard similar comments.

For a variety of reasons, many of us find ourselves isolated from, or choosing to isolate ourselves from, those who don't share our commitment to Jesus. We don't spend much time with them and aren't comfortable talking with them about important issues. Yet we keep wishing that somehow, sometime, we might introduce someone to a personal relationship with Christ. We are caught between what we read in 2 Corinthians 6:17—"Therefore come out from them and be separate"—and John 17:18 and Matthew 5:14, where Jesus says he has "sent" his disciples into the world and calls them "the light of the world."

What Holds Us Back?

Why don't we spend more time cultivating relationships outside our Christian circles? Only when we face our obstacles and excuses honestly can we focus on making new choices that will enable us to create and nurture life-transforming relationships that have eternal value.

Lack of time. Many of us are so busy that it's difficult to carve out time for one more thing or person, especially someone whose challenges concerning Christianity might require hours of ongoing discussion and even research, or at least risk taking and vulnerability. I face this issue often and wrestle with what my time commitments should be. When I'm really honest, I realize I usually find time for things I want to do and for urgent things that scream for attention. Sometimes I even get to the important things, which usually don't clamor for attention. In *The Life You've Always Wanted,* John Ortberg writes about what he calls "hurry sickness" and how it hinders us from loving God and loving people. How many times have I missed opportunities because I'm just too busy?

A related problem is that we simply don't know many (or any) folks outside our church circles. Recently pastors in two different states told me that they'd like to spend time with non-Christians but can't. "I'm in so many meetings and helping so many church people," one said, "that I don't have time to go out and meet non-Christians."

For years I've been haunted by a strange notion. What if all the pastors and youth group leaders in this country stood up this coming Sunday and said, "I want to ask you two personal questions, and you have to be truthful. How many of you have meaningful interaction concerning your faith with at least one non-Christian every week? And how many of you regularly ask God to give you non-Christian friends?" How many hands do you think would go up?

For many of us, knowing non-Christians is not a priority. We don't want people to die without knowing Jesus personally, but it's all too easy for us to remain indifferent to (and even unaware of) the responsibilities God has given us concerning the lives of people around us. They simply may never have seen the love of Jesus demonstrated to them or never have read about the Jesus who came to earth, died and was resurrected.

As harsh as this may sound, many of us place a low priority on cultivating meaningful relationships with non-Christians and sharing the light of Jesus because we don't think much about heaven and hell—and what it would be like to spend eternity in hell. Hell and sin are not popular discussion topics in our culture, where words like *community* and *tolerance* rule. They are not even popular topics in many churches or in widely read Christian books. Sadly, we also tend to live as if we were not citizens of heaven, pursuing many earthly goals and objectives, valuing our titles, possessions and reputations more than we hunger to be obedient disciples of Jesus.

Hey, you may be thinking, *I work with non-Christians every day*. If so, you are in a great place to share what Jesus is doing in your life, and I hope some points in this book will encourage you to do this if you aren't already.

OVER-THE-FENCE TALK

This method of meeting people has been happening for centuries, and it still works. Noah certainly met his neighbors when he was building the 450-foot-long ark. Abraham met three men while he was sitting at the door of his tent to escape the heat (Genesis 18:1-2). Rebekah met Isaac in a field and ended up marrying him (Genesis 24:62-66). Jacob met Rachel at the mouth of a well, a gathering place for shepherds (Genesis 29:7-12).

The next time a neighbor you seldom see is doing an outside chore, chasing an errant child or just sitting on a porch sipping a cold drink, walk over and say hello. (Yes, this works even when there are no fences, only parking lots.)

Ron and Susan, whom we met "over a fence" more than twenty years ago, came over for dinner again the other evening. We moved miles away from them years ago, but we still stay in close touch. Recently we gave them a New Testament devotional product that we compiled, and Susan is reading it.

If we're honest, some of us must admit that we are unwilling or unable to share what Jesus means to us. In this age of so-called spiritual tolerance, when people expect everybody else to give them the freedom to believe pretty much whatever they want to believe, it's easy to give in to the temptation to say little or nothing about Jesus. We may not want to upset others. Or perhaps we haven't been able to articulate what we believe even to ourselves. Or, as has happened to me, we realize deep inside that our relationship with God doesn't always match our professed belief.

Years ago I worked as a magazine editor for an organization in Washington, D.C. Even though I sometimes spoke of Jesus with people I met on the bus riding to work, it was as if I turned off that switch when I got to the office. I did what was expected of me, worked hard and left. I found it easy to chat with coworkers about almost everything but what God was doing in my life.

I had set up a false dichotomy that separated my workday world from the rest of my world. Instead of viewing all of life as spiritual and using opportunities I had to gently share the relevance of God and the Bible at appropriate times, I kept my faith inside. Instead of creating curiosity about my faith and explaining more when coworkers asked questions, I compartmentalized.

Fear. I'm amazed at how often fear raises its ugly head within me. Fear can carry over into my relationships with others unless I focus more on God than on myself. My fearful thoughts go like this: *I don't want to offend. What if I ask the wrong question? How can I say something when this person knows I face similar struggles? What if I don't have the right words to say, or I say the wrong words? Am I being hypocritical if I talk about the love of God when I'm not feeling it right now? What if sharing something about my spiritual life hurts my relationship with this person? Is this the best time to say something? Have I really earned the right to speak to him or her?*

In the midst of such fears and rationalizations, it's easy to leave "evan-

Over the years, I have watched many longtime Christians who have attended church for twenty or thirty years smugly judge and condemn those who have not stepped over the boundary line by praying the sinner's prayer. The questions need to be asked, How do you know that the person outside is not moving toward Christ? How do you know that you haven't spent the last decade moving away from him?

RICH NATHAN

gelism" to someone who is "more gifted in that area" rather than remembering that God wants to use who we are and the resources he has given us to bring the light of Christ into our circles of influence. It's not easy to grasp 2 Corinthians 5:20: "We are therefore Christ's ambassadors, as though God were making his appeal through us."

Many times I wonder why God would choose to use me as his ambassador. I go through times of doubt. I choose to sin. I am not gifted in a number of areas. I can't even begin to keep up with relationships that are important to me, much less all the reading I want to do. Yet during those moments when I rest in God's presence, I realize it's all okay. He doesn't want me to be Superman or to pretend I'm perfect. He just wants me—a tall guy with skinny legs who had to drop a philosophy class or risk flunking it—to walk with him and reflect his love and truth to others.

THE MORE INSIDIOUS REASON

As real as these reasons are, I believe there is an even deeper and sometimes unconscious reason why we insulate and isolate ourselves from people outside the church. This powerful reason is at the root of our frequent failure to befriend people and share Jesus' love and truth with them. It has to do with stereotypes.

Jesus was no stranger to stereotypes. During his ministry, he encountered many stereotypes of what the Messiah was supposed to be and do. His disciples, and some Roman authorities, expected him to take political control by force. Religious leaders criticized him for eating with "sinners." (Their Messiah would not stoop that low!) Crowds of people left him when they realized that being his follower wouldn't be easy (John 6:66). People challenged how he, a common carpenter's son, could claim to be the Christ.

The images of the Messiah were so strong that many people were unable to recognize Jesus for who he was.

Most of us stereotype people too. To see what I mean, try an experiment with me.

Which words or images come to mind when you read each of these words: *lumberjack, exotic dancer, Muslim, Jew, agnostic, preacher, real-estate developer, writer?* How does each person dress? How does each treat people? What does each do in his or her free time?

Now let's take this a step closer to the topic of this chapter. Which words or images come to mind when you read the word *non-Christian?*

BE A FRIEND

When Stan first transferred into the high school Cory Hardesty attended, nobody talked to him. So Cory introduced himself and ended up showing Stan how to play football and helping him meet other students.

"Even though Stan became really popular," Cory says, "he and I remained connected because I was the first person to befriend him."

Cory transferred to a different high school after his sophomore year but stayed in touch with Stan intentionally by going to football and basketball games in which Stan was playing and going out with the team afterward.

One night Cory invited Stan to attend a church youth group, but he didn't come. So Cory invited him several more times. "He showed up one week," Cory says, "and found Christ that night. The next week he brought two more people. The next week he brought even more."

Then Stan's parents started attending Cory's church, and both of them became Christians. Stan's aunts and uncles started visiting.

"In my senior year I began discipling Stan," Cory says. "We remained closely connected during college and then ended up being roommates. Today he is still on fire for God, speaking to youth and involved in ministry."

Perhaps you respond to it with such words as *seeker, pagan, unbeliever, anti-Christian, lost soul*. Or maybe you thought of words like *Buddhist, humanist, antichurch, anti-Bible* . . .

There's no right or wrong answer here. The point is, we all associate images with certain words and respond accordingly.

The dictionary defines a *stereotype* as a standardized image or concept to which we give special meaning and that is held in common by people in a group.

Stereotypes can be helpful. They aid us in categorizing objects and people—in preparing to encounter them, determining how we will respond to them, figuring out where we will store information about them and how we will evaluate that information, and determining the experiences we desire (or don't desire) to have with them. So talking about getting rid of stereotypes completely is nonsense. But stereotypes also hinder or completely block our outreach beyond the church if we are not careful.

Fewer and fewer people in the Western world are turning to Christ or even viewing Christianity as a viable alternative worldview. And one reason is, many Christians have negative stereotypes of what non-Christians are like and respond accordingly. For example, to some Christians, non-Christians are the enemy—proponents of views that challenge the entire Christian worldview. To others, non-Christians are pagans who haven't given the Christian worldview an intellectual chance. Yet other Christians consider non-Christians to be people "of the world"—supporters of sinful perspectives that threaten the family unit and the foundation of morality—and therefore are to be avoided or at least aggressively challenged.

There are many reasons for these sorts of negative stereotypes. I've heard preachers condemn those who don't believe in Jesus, and that viewpoint certainly influences people in the pews. I've read books in which non-Christians are labeled unfairly. I've heard that non-Christians will lead us to hell. (Yes, some non-Christians advocate and promote beliefs and practices that are incompatible with what the Bible teaches. But aren't we Christians guilty of doing such things as well? Isn't that what God's grace and forgiveness are all about?)

As Linda Wright asks in her book *Christianity's Crisis in Evangelism:*

> Have all non-Christians made *conscious* choices to defy God? Are they necessarily and overtly anti-God and out to destroy us—or have sloppy thinking and unexamined prejudices about life distorted our perceptions? . . . Have we opted for the easier route of putting everyone in categories so we don't have to do the work of finding out where they are and what our responsibility is to them?

These days quite a few of my friends are not Christians. What I've learned during many delightful hours with them has changed the way I think about them. To my surprise, I've come to realize that I have much more in common with them than I used to think I did. This realization has led me to believe that bad stereotyping is a key reason Christians fail to develop meaningful relationships with non-Christians.

I've wondered, painfully sometimes, how many non-Christians I chose to ignore or didn't love fully, consciously or unconsciously, because of stereotypes I used to have or ones that still clamor for prominence in my mind and heart today.

Here are some generalized things I have discovered about many singles and couples who don't currently claim relationship to Christ:

- They are family oriented and love children. Whether they are in their first or second marriage, they work at strengthening their relationships with their spouses. If they are single, they are loyal to friends and family members.

- They work long hours, in and out of the home, and highly value recreation. They read books, play games, go to movies, hike, ski, do woodworking, fish, hunt and share laughter over meals with family and friends.

- They struggle with finances sometimes and watch how they spend money. They face illness and death, get lonely, make mistakes and suffer consequences, and get sore muscles. They grumble about the weather and get angry about child pornography.

- They wrestle with such issues as abortion, support for public versus private schools, violence in the media and why health insurance costs so much.

- They have favorite pets, want to be accepted and loved for who they are, and search for genuine intimacy—to know and be known. They plan for the future, try to live authentically in the present and are overcoming "emotional baggage" from the past.

- They are kind and compassionate, can't figure out why God allows such suffering in the world and like to keep some spiritual topics mostly private. They want to find peace and hope but don't like being pressured to find them in a certain religion. They want to reach their own conclusions about spirituality.

- They love to laugh. But sometimes crying feels good too.

As I reflect on my life, I'm struck by how many times non-Christians have loved and cared for my family and met our needs—and still do. They volunteer to keep our computers working so we can do our editorial work. They fix our cars. They kept me company as I lay in bed for months recovering from back surgery and remain a phone call away if I need help lifting something heavy. They invite us over for meals, encourage our daughter and enrich our lives in many other ways too numerous to list here. Just last night and into the early-morning hours of today, one of them helped to keep a chimney fire in our home from spreading.

Having realized at last that I have much more in common with non-Christians than I had ever thought or had been taught, I've discovered that non-Christians have many things in common with Christians on a spiritual level too. The only difference is that we are no longer "slaves" to sin (Romans 6:20-22) and have been forgiven of our sins

(1 John 1:9). God has given us his gifts of salvation, the fruit of the Spirit, the power we need to be his ambassadors, the deep joy and peace only he can provide.

Like us, non-Christians are born sinful, are separated from God and need forgiveness through the blood of Christ. They are created in the image of God, and Christ died for them.

They are influenced by Satan, who seeks to keep them spiritually blind. They battle with sin (although they may not call it "sin"). They have a deep hunger for spiritual fulfillment, even if some of them do not yet recognize it.

They have unique, God-given abilities, talents, dreams and desires. They face temptations, make mistakes and need to hear God's Word. They wish bad things didn't happen in the world—and in their neighborhoods.

LANGUAGE STEREOTYPES

It wasn't easy for me to grasp the fact that non-Christians are quite similar to me in many ways. I never heard anyone address this issue as I grew up attending Sunday school and church. And to this day, I've never heard a pastor preach on this subject.

What might people (non-Christians *and* Christians) think if they saw this sermon title in bold letters on a church sign: "Non-Christians Are Like Us in So Many Ways"?

It's vital for Christians to realize that these similarities exist and begin breaking down stereotypes of non-Christians so we can respond to them warmly as people for whom Jesus died, people he loves, people he calls us to love, people who can give much to us and to whom we can give much. Otherwise, the *us* and *them* barrier remains.

Language itself promotes stereotypes of people, including non-Christians. Consider, for example, a few words that are commonly used to refer to people who have not received Jesus Christ as their Lord and Savior. Unfortunately, there are problems associated with each word or phrase.

Common Words	Problems with These Words
unbelievers	Many people who are not Christians have strong beliefs. They just don't believe what Christians believe.
seekers	Many people who are not Christians are quite content with their spirituality or lack thereof and are not seeking spiritual things. (On the other hand, those who are seeking spirituality that's not biblical are at least seeking, so this term fits them.)
pre-Christians	Implies that people who are not Christians will respond to Christ if they hear the gospel. Many will not, especially as adults.
the lost	Implies that someone who is not a Christian is wayward or confused. Many non-Christians are confident of their direction, although they have not chosen the way to God through Jesus.
people	We could just use words such as this (or "another person" or "the other person"), but then we'll always have to qualify which one(s).
non-Christians	This term fits a biblical definition but offends people who believe they are Christians by birth, family upbringing and so on. It also defines people by what they are not. ("I'm not Buddhist or Jewish; I'm Christian.") Seems to be the best option so far, so I'm using it in this book. If you have a better one, please let me know.
OtherThanChristian	I made this one up but realized that it's far too cumbersome and creates an "us-them" barrier. (Guess I could use OTC as an abbreviation, but people would think it referred to something like Officers Training Corps.)

This simple chart illustrates how pervasive our stereotypes are and how they hinder our communication with those who are not Christians. It's even difficult to know which words to use to refer to non-Christians! But we need to wrestle with this, because our words reveal how we think and what we believe—and speak volumes to a watching, listening, increasingly secularized audience.

If you find yourself squirming, relax. This chapter isn't meant to produce guilt. These points challenge me. There aren't easy answers, but that doesn't mean we should avoid the struggle.

During recent years, God has certainly made it clear that he wants to use me to connect with non-Christians. A cultural gulf is widening between Christians and non-Christians, and that concerns me because God still calls us to be salt and light in our world. He still calls us to share his love with people in relevant ways. To reveal his truth. To demonstrate the   Bible's relevance at work, at school, in our neighborhoods. To live in obedience to him and in the process guide others toward him. To love other people as we love ourselves. And we can't, and won't, do these things as long as we hold on to, and live according to, false, stereotypical perceptions of non-Christians.

STEREOTYPES OF CHRISTIANS

So far I've written about Christians' stereotypes and their impact. But there's another factor we need to figure in. The other side of the stereotype coin has to do with non-Christians' perceptions of what Christians are like. As I'm sure you realize from listening to non-Christians you've met, many of them have stereotypical views of Jesus, Christians, the Bible and Christianity.

My friend Howard once said to me, "Christians can't defend why they believe what they believe so they appeal to 'faith.'"

Carol, who I met at a neighbor's birthday party, discovered I was a Christian and asked, "Why do Christians make such a big deal about the church services and prayer meetings they attend? It seems to me they are just trying to prove that they are better than the rest of us, and that's not true."

Rick and Janice, who lived near a large church, noticed that people driving into and out of the church's parking lot drove aggressively and often wouldn't let them change lanes so they could get home. "Christians aren't nice people," they concluded.

BUILD HUMOR INTO THE PICTURE

Some people think that Christians are just stick-in-the-muds who don't know how to have a good time. Prove them wrong. Rent a truly funny comedy, pull out a great game and invite new friends over to your home.

Bob, a longtime friend, said to me, "Christians talk about love, but they fight all the time about denominational differences and which Bible translations are accurate."

An attorney I know is deathly afraid of Christians. "They are always trying to get into positions of power from which they can legislate what is right and wrong and tell me how to think," he said to me one evening. "What gives them the corner on truth?"

Quite often I wonder what non-Christians think about Christians when a car with bumper stickers about God's love cuts me off. Or when I see people carrying "God is love" placards blocking the walkway on Bourbon Street in New Orleans. Or when I hear Christians publicly denouncing movies they haven't seen. Or when I meet people who have renounced Christianity because Christians spoke a lot about forgiveness but were the last ones to offer it. Or when I see someone in a mall wearing a T-shirt or hat with an in-your-face slogan ridiculing anybody who doesn't believe in Jesus or the Bible.

I can see why some non-Christians have negative stereotypes of Christians! We are not always an attractive bunch.

A song I've often heard on the radio has lyrics similar to these: "We may be going to hell, but at least we're enjoying the ride." What are those band members trying to communicate?

Sadly, for a number of non-Christians, words such as *Christians, church* and *Bible* are loaded with negative connotations. For them those words simply don't bring to mind positive connotations such as *love, relationship, community, acceptance, healing, truth, kindness* and *lasting peace.*

What do non-Christians think of when they hear or read the word *church?* Do they think of a preacher they saw on television preaching damnation or talking about truth that everybody is supposed to believe—or else? Or people who talk about love but aren't loving? Or the building some fancy-dressed people enter every week after ignoring nearby street people? Or remember a time when they did go inside a church but nobody paid any attention to them or they heard that being good isn't enough to get into heaven and little else that made sense?

I've met far too many non-Christians who view the church as a place where a preacher talks about things they don't agree with or even understand and where there's a whole list of unspoken rules and dress codes. It's also a place where hidden agendas lurk ("Come to the Easter program and learn that Jesus rose from the dead"). Little wonder that many non-Christians choose to allocate little time for the organized church, or spiritual things in general.

Last week a neighbor joined us for dinner. In passing, I made a general statement about spirituality to see what he might say. Immediately he responded, "Spirituality is for people who have too much time on their hands." Then he changed the subject. This is the same guy who plowed our road after the last snowstorm.

Several weeks ago the daughter of a good friend of mine invited a non-Christian teenager to attend church with her. He went, but toward the end of the service he felt so frustrated that tears came to his eyes. Having never been taught anything about God and the Bible, he simply could not understand what was going on. Everything was foreign to him. Fortunately he was able to express his frustrations later and get some questions answered, before he formed stereotypes that might have stuck with him the rest of his life.

In the next chapter we'll look at why it's important for us to express sincere love toward non-Christians and what impact such love can have.

FOR REFLECTION AND DISCUSSION

These questions, and those at the end of each chapter in this book, are designed to help you consider and discuss key points and how they apply to daily life. The questions are appropriate for a person reading this book alone or for a group such as a Sunday school class or a retreat small group. If you're using this book with a group, you'll want to look through appendix two, "Leading and Promoting Group Discussion."

1. On a scale of 1 to 10 (1 = having no significant contact with non-Christians; 10 = being in active contact with them), which number would you give yourself? Why?

2. Looking back on your life so far, how have your stereotypes influenced the degree to which you have reflected Christ's love and truth to non-Christians?

3. How did you feel when you answered what the word *non-Christian* means to you? Why?

4. In what way(s) have you tried to isolate yourself from non-Christians? Or, in contrast, what have you done in the past to build relationships with them? What happened as a result?

5. What did you first think when you read that in many ways Christians are like non-Christians? Why? (Be honest.)

6. Pretend you are a non-Christian, looking at Christians and their subculture, including community interaction and church meetings. Which things are attractive? Which things aren't?

7. Which practical action(s) might you begin to take now in order to meet and befriend non-Christians in ways that will expose them to Jesus' love, biblical truth and the community of loving Christians?

8. What do you see the church doing to break down stereotypes of non-Christians? How do you see the church perpetuating those stereotypes?

— 2 —

Cultivating Sincere Love

We were gentle among you, like a mother caring for her little children.

We loved you so much that we were delighted to share with you not only

the gospel of God but our lives as well.

PAUL (1 THESSALONIANS 2:7-8, EMPHASIS ADDED)

Deep, sacrificial, unconditional love was at the heart of everything Jesus did on earth. A prayer he prayed just before his crucifixion reveals the legacy of love he left us: "Righteous Father, though the world does not know you, I know you, and they know that you have sent me. I have made you known to them, and will continue to make you known in or- der that *the love you have for me may be in them* and that I myself may be in them" (John 17:25-26, emphasis added).

Think of it: we have inside of us the same love that God the Father has for his Son! And everywhere we go, we have opportunities to express this love.

One afternoon as I walked out of a mall after seeing a movie, I felt a burden for people around me who didn't know God and a renewed de- sire to allow God to work through me. I seldom pray while walking in a mall parking lot, but this time I did. *God, please help me stand for you. I want to connect with people in ways that make a difference for your kingdom.*

Approaching my car, which I'd parked *way* out in the lot so nobody would bang a car door into it, I noticed a pickup truck nearby. A man was sitting inside the hood. *Not now, God,* I objected quickly. *I do want to help somebody, but this isn't the best time for me.*

I had several choices: (1) get into my car as quickly as possible and drive away, (2) walk over, show mild interest and then leave without saying much or (3) sincerely ask if I could help and then stick around. (At this point you need to know that I'm not a mechanic. I'm a pretty good troubleshooter because I've had to keep various high-mileage cars and trucks running on a tight budget. But I still have parts in our garage left over from repairs, or attempted repairs, on vehicles I no longer own.)

When I asked, "Can I help you?" I was not feeling "spiritual." In fact I was hoping he'd say, "No, using your license-plate number, my in-dash laptop computer brought up a skills-and-aptitude profile of you that indicates you'll do more harm than good if you lift a finger or tool to help me. Thanks anyway." But he didn't. He invited me to help.

So I started cranking the starter when he asked me to, and in between cranks he began talking. He told me that he'd done lots of wrong things but had worked with a Christian in his previous job. Now unemployed with little money, he was traveling to where he hoped a job was waiting. When I mentioned I was a Christian, he began asking about Jesus' love and forgiveness, and soon the discussion centered on the Bible. He expressed interest in reading it but said he didn't own a copy.

As it turned out, I *was* able to help him repair his truck. I helped him borrow several tools from a nearby shop, talked through repair options with him, and cranked the starter over and over until finally he got the distributor adjustment right and the engine started. (I never told him about the prayer I had uttered with great sincerity two minutes earlier: *God, I don't think this battery has more than about two more cranks in it. And I'm really late for my meeting. So if you want to get this guy on the road again, now would be a good time to help us out.*)

I offered to buy him dinner, but he didn't have time. After he left to return the borrowed tools, I placed a note and money for a Bible or a meal on his steering wheel. When I got home, my daughter asked, "Did you help a guy in a parking lot?" He had called my home to thank me.

Most likely I'll never see or hear from him again. But that afternoon I had recognized God's appointment for me. I was reminded that God wants to use me in even the most ordinary places and situations. I also couldn't help but reflect on the fact that I'm often too busy and self-focused to hear what God is saying. (What if when I get to heaven, God shows me a graph indicating the people he placed in my path and the times I walked right by them instead of speaking to them?) So I'm working on this area.

LOVE IS MOST IMPORTANT

I feel good inside when I'm the recipient of someone's sincere, genuine love. Don't you? God's love for us, our love for him and the love he gives us for other people are essential to the Christian life. Love is the key to building relationships with non-Christians and breaking down stereotypes. The apostle Paul described love this way in 1 Corinthians 13, a chapter you may be quite familiar with.

> Love is patient, love is kind. It does not envy, it does not boast, it is not proud. It is not rude, it is not self-seeking, it is not easily angered, it keeps no record of wrongs. Love does not delight in evil but rejoices with the truth. It always protects, always trusts, always hopes, always perseveres. Love never fails. . . . And now these three remain: faith, hope and love. But the greatest of these is love. (1 Corinthians 13:4-8, 13)

When we love people with this kind of God-given, God-enabled love, they know it. They may not respond to our love right away, or ever. They may never acknowledge it. They may question its validity or find a way to rationalize away our motives. But this kind of love penetrates past the thickest skin, to the core of people's hearts and minds.

This is especially true when seeking people realize that Jesus, who is

PASS ALONG A COMPLIMENT

Solomon wrote, "How good is a timely word!" (Proverbs 15:23). A cheerful word can still open doors to relationships, even in our impersonal society. For a while, nearly every time I drove past a certain house down the road from us, I noticed that an improvement had been made. The trash disappeared. A new picnic area sprouted. The house was repainted. And so on.

One afternoon, as I returned from the park with my German shepherd, I noticed a man and woman standing in the front yard of that home. I stopped my pickup and walked back to say hello. The couple looked at my jeans and dog and offered a tepid, unenthusiastic "Hi." (Translation: "What are you doing here? What do you want? Do we know you?")

"I just wanted to tell you that I think you're doing a great job with this house," I said. "It's really looking good." Immediately their faces beamed. We talked for nearly twenty minutes, and I later enjoyed a meal with them before they moved to another state.

Truth incarnate, also is Love incarnate. After watching Mel Gibson's movie *The Passion of the Christ,* many filmgoers simply remained silent in their seats, trying to grasp the impact of what they had just seen. Some people, no doubt, were surprised to discover that love is not simply an ideal built around the Golden Rule. Jesus is love, and he demonstrated that by becoming a person just like us and dying a horrible death for us. During the film's run in theaters, millions of people were exposed to the biblical truth that Jesus died for each one of them because of their sin. During the film's last few seconds, they were also challenged to remember that he rose from the dead and still has nailprints in his hands—permanent evidences of his love.

Even quite ordinary people can be powerful carriers of God's love.

RANDY RAYSBROOK'S STORY

Having been disillusioned with the externalized Christianity he encountered in Catholic prep school, Randy completely abandoned religion when he started college and immersed himself in fraternity decadence. God and religion meant nothing to him. One day he heard a guy named Hal Lindsey talk about biblical end times in a fraternity house and was intellectually intrigued when Hal explained verses from the book of Matthew. Randy continued to party regularly after that, but intuitively he knew that the Bible was God's Word. *If a man had a Bible and could lean on this,* he thought, *he could endure anything.*

Quitting school at the end of his junior year, Randy became a policeman in California, then in Oregon, and launched a spiritual search. These are his words:

> I visited a Mormon church. I wanted God and knew there was more about him I didn't know. Eventually I moved my girlfriend to Oregon; we lived together for a year and a half. Although I was a cop, I was abusive to women I lived with and dated. Because I stuffed my emotions, I was great in crisis situations. I could watch people dying and be disengaged emotionally.
>
> I broke up with my girlfriend and started dating a woman who attended an evangelical church. (I started going to church because of her.) Everett, the pastor, surprised me. He had strong convictions, and I wasn't used to seeing a man like that in the pulpit. He wasn't afraid to confront people on issues, wasn't afraid to speak biblical truth that might offend people. He was rough around the edges, but he loved the Bible and shared the gospel in virtually every message.
>
> Gradually he started to build a relationship with me. The men in the church also started asking me to barbecues. They were loggers and ranchers—men I looked up to because I liked that lifestyle. They all seemed like real, whole people who had no artificial agendas.

To learn more about God, I started going to Bible study on Wednesday nights. As Everett went through Bible passages, I argued with him constantly. I was combative and rude. But no matter how forceful I'd be, he kept loving me. He'd say, "Let's talk about that. Have you looked at this? What about this Bible verse?" He knew the Scriptures well and used them effectively. When I gave him my strongest objections, he didn't back down. He didn't change his mind because I didn't agree with him. He wasn't a wimp. Nor was he condescending or patronizing. He won my respect; that was key for me. As a cop, I believed if you didn't have respect you didn't have anything.

Everett just loved me. He started inviting me over to his house for dinner, and I remember saying to him, "If you ever try to force this Bible stuff on me, I'm out the back door." I put him on notice that he wasn't going to get me to do anything. Yet he kept coming back. I'd resist and argue, but he was unflinching in his pursuit of me. He kept inviting me to do things with him and was wise enough to keep shooting straight with me.

Slowly something started happening inside Randy. Because of the love he was seeing, he hungered to learn more about the Bible and hear it explained. About ten months later, he realized he was a sinner but God loved him and would forgive him in spite of the way he'd lived. Soon afterward he became a Christian. God gave him a new heart and mind, from which flowed sincere love and a new way of relating to others.

Today, on staff with The Navigators, Randy does evangelism and discipleship training, develops evangelism and discipleship tools, and teaches at two universities. He still remembers the love he received from Christians in that small Oregon town. "Today," he says, "I try to reach out in love to other people the way Everett and those men in Oregon reached out to me. If I do that, God is glorified regardless of how someone responds. The question I try to ask myself is, *Am I trying to love each person with a pure heart?* If so, God is pleased."

THE IMPACT OF LOVE

Over and over again Jesus emphasized the impact of love: "A new command I give you: Love one another. As I have loved you, so you must love one another. By this all men will know that you are my disciples, *if you love one another*" (John 13:34-35, emphasis added). Notice that he didn't say, "They will know if you debate them, give them things, pressure them, have the right church programs for each segment of the congregation . . ."

How many there are who . . . have lost their light and their joy! They were once burning and shining lights in the family, in the Sunday school, and in the church. But something has come between them and God—the world or self—and their light has gone out. Reader, if you are one who has had this experience, may God help you to come back to the altar of the Savior's love and light up your torch anew, so that you can go out into the lanes and alleys and let the light of the gospel shine in these dark homes.

Jesus loved everybody around him, including religious leaders whose hypocrisy, deceit and false teaching angered him. He loved the unwashed, the scoundrels, the despised, the lonely, the people trapped in terrible sin. He chose to love even the most undesirable people rather than pulling away in disgust. He expressed love to people in their homes and in the marketplaces. He didn't just wait for them to walk into the synagogue. He spent time with influential people yet enjoyed the company of common folks. He lived out what he preached, *showing* as well as *telling* the love of God.

Did Jesus demonstrate such deep, all-encompassing love because he is the Son of God and it is part of his nature to love? Yes, but I think something else is going on too. Jesus loves all people, including non-Christians. He knows their deepest emotions. He knows their thoughts. He doesn't want them to wander through life without their Shepherd. He doesn't want them to face eternity in hell. Better than anyone, he knows

DWIGHT L. MOODY

what a blessed relationship with God is really like and doesn't want anyone to miss out. And he calls us—those who have invited him to be the Lord and Savior of our lives—to express that same love to others.

JESUS LOVES UNCONDITIONALLY

How easy it is for me to help people who are grateful for my help and, conversely, to overlook people who don't seem to appreciate it. But Jesus loved people even when he *knew* that his love would be scorned or unappreciated.

After a leper begged, on his knees, for healing, Jesus healed him but warned him not to tell anyone. So what did the healed man immediately do? "He went out and began to talk freely, spreading the news" (Mark 1:45). As a result, Jesus could no longer enter towns openly.

When Jesus went to Jairus's home after the synagogue ruler's daughter had died, he told mourners that she was only asleep. Their response? "They laughed at him" (Mark 5:40). His response? He shooed them out of the house and healed the girl.

Ten lepers called out to Jesus, "Jesus, Master, have pity on us!" So he told them to show themselves to the priests, who could certify healing. "As they went, they were cleansed," Luke reports. But only one, a Samaritan, came back to praise God and thank Jesus. Did Jesus know ahead of

---

ASK GOD FOR SENSITIVITY TO HURTING PEOPLE

People all around us are hurting. Marriages crumble. People lose their jobs. Illnesses strike without warning. If we are willing to provide a listening ear and practical help, we can show non-Christians that we really do care about them.

What about taking a meal to someone, driving him or her to a doctor's appointment, dropping off some videos for someone who is recuperating? Sometimes the most simple kindnesses help us earn the right to speak God's truth.

time that nine of the healed men wouldn't return? You bet. (See Luke 17:11-19.)

Of course it's not always easy to love non-Christians. They can be antagonistic toward Christians and the gospel. They can delight in pursuing sinful pleasures. They can be offensive or defensive when approached by anyone who claims to have "spiritual truth." I have participated in small group meetings in which others railed against Christians and did their best to put me on the defensive.

Yet Christ commands us to love such people and do whatever we can to share the gospel with them. Just as God made Paul "a light for the Gentiles" (Acts 13:47), he has called us to reach those who do not yet know him personally. And I believe the most effective proclamation of the gospel occurs within the context of a loving relationship.

It seems incontrovertible that if we are even to begin to follow the real Jesus, and to walk in his shoes, we must seize every opportunity to "do good." Our good works will show the genuineness of our love, and our love will show the genuineness of our faith.

JOHN R. W. STOTT

One criticism often leveled at Christians is that we tend to quarrel and argue with non-Christians rather than listening respectfully to their viewpoints and finding areas of common ground with them. We respond as if we have all the answers rather than being open to hearing new perspectives and admitting we are still on a spiritual journey. Regretfully, I've done my share of arguing.

Years ago I began meeting with adherents of the Baha'i religion and discussing how their beliefs differed from the Bible's teachings. The more I read in preparation, the more I noticed rational inconsistencies in the Baha'i religion. Secretly I became proud of my "apologetics" approach that could target weaknesses in the Baha'i faith.

While studying at a prestigious college, a young man who had grown up in our neighborhood had become interested in Baha'i. One day we started talking, and instead of listening to his views I quickly blasted the weaknesses of Baha'i. He stopped talking, and we never reestablished genuine connection. Not only had I slammed the faith he was investigating, I had carelessly damaged his dignity by implying that anyone who pursued Baha'i hadn't examined the facts and their implications.

It's challenging to patiently love people who stridently express negative views about Christian faith, views that are based on false reasoning, emotion, bad experiences they have had or beliefs they have honed for years. It can be hard to love people who call loudly for religious tolerance and yet have little or no tolerance for Christians and their beliefs. When we encounter such people, it's especially important to remember how Jesus lovingly meets people. When I met Jesus, I sure needed his loving acceptance and forgiveness. And I still do!

JESUS WENT OUT OF HIS WAY TO BUILD RELATIONSHIPS

Jesus was a master communicator. Sometimes he talked with intellectuals like Nicodemus, answering questions but always sticking to biblical truth. Sometimes he talked with prostitutes and beggars whose only education was on-the-job training in "Four Ways to Make Your Voice Heard over a Crowd," "How to Stretch Your Income with Effective Hand Gestures and Voice Intonations" and "Ways to Adapt Your Appearance to Achieve Maximum Marketing Results from Passersby." Jesus continually looked for ways to reach out to people and connect with them.

> Jesus entered Jericho and was passing through. A man was there by the name of Zacchaeus; he was a chief tax collector and was wealthy. He wanted to see who Jesus was, but being a short man he could not, because of the crowd. So he ran ahead and climbed a sycamore-fig tree to see him, since Jesus was coming that way.
>
> When Jesus reached the spot, he looked up and said to him, "Zacchaeus, come down immediately. I must stay at your house today." So he came down at once and welcomed him gladly. (Luke 19:1-6)

Everywhere he went, Jesus recognized people who needed him and tried to build authentic relationships with them, even when it meant calling them out of trees! Today we also have great opportunities to build relationships with non-Christians.

Recently I attended a ballet recital in which the thirteen-year-old daughter of a new friend danced in key scenes. Do I know a *grand battement* from a *relevé?* No. Could I tell how someone executed a complicated move or which was most difficult? No. And to be perfectly honest, watching ballet is not one of my favorite pastimes. I went because my new friend and his wife invited my wife and me to participate with his family in something that is important to them. And I had a surprisingly good time.

Sometimes it's as if non-Christians are saying to us, "*Show me* that you really care about me! Invite me to go cycling with you. Show up at the hospital when my daughter has surgery. Lend me a book that has been special to you. Invite me to see a movie with you. Notice when I'm feeling down. Invite me to walk with you. Call me to say hello. Lend me a tool I need."

We are called . . . to mirror the love of God—a love that is so extravagant that we must never keep it to ourselves. We must spread it around. It is not a mushy love, all sentiment and no action. Jesus' love drove him deeply into the lives of people. He cared for their wholeness. When he went out into a day, he did not ask himself, Is this my social action day, or do I give them the salvation message? Jesus cared for people as he found them. So must we care for their wholeness—spiritual, social, psychological, you name it.

REBECCA MANLEY PIPPERT

Yes, demonstrating love that encourages relationship takes time. And the spiritual reward may not come for many years—or even during our lifetimes. A friend told me that for four years she walked an hour a day with a non-Christian woman. The woman never became a Christian during that time, but she sure learned a lot about God and how he helped meet my friend's needs.

God calls us to cultivate genuine, loving relationships with non-Christians and to seek to *be* loving people. That's a tall order. Charles Colson reminds us, "We must not merely assent mentally to certain principles; we must *become* people who are just, courageous, patient, kind, loyal, loving, persistent, and devoted to duty."

JESUS RESPONDED WITH COMPASSION

The dictionary defines *compassion* as "a feeling of deep empathy . . . for another who is stricken by misfortune, accompanied by a strong desire to alleviate the suffering." Although many of us don't use the word *compassion* much in normal conversation, Jesus exuded this quality. "When he saw the crowds, he had compassion on them, because they were harassed and helpless" (Matthew 9:36). Speaking to his disciples, he said, "I have compassion for these people; they have already been with me three days and have nothing to eat" (Matthew 15:32). Why did he reach out his hand and touch the leper? He was "filled with compassion" (Mark 1:41). The Greek word translated *compassion* in these verses means "to have pity, to feel sympathy with or for someone."

When Jesus saw Mary weeping after her brother's death, and the people with her also weeping, he wept (John 11:35). "As he approached Jerusalem and saw the city, he wept over it and said, 'If you, even you, had only known on this day what would bring you peace—but now it is hidden from your eyes'" (Luke 19:41-42).

The Bible clearly states that we are to show genuine compassion, especially for widows, orphans, strangers, prisoners, and people who are hungry and thirsty and need clothing (see Matthew 25:35-36; James 1:27). Paul urges, "Clothe yourselves with compassion" (Colossians 3:12).

Because of our love for God and what he has done for us, we are to obey him: "This is love for God: to obey his commands" (1 John 5:3). When God commanded us to love one another, he knew we could do it. Likewise, if we ask him to lead us to people who need to experience his love through us, he will do it! It may lead to inconvenience and redistribution of our dollars and time, but acts of compassion connect powerfully with non-Christians (and Christians too). Love makes an especially powerful connection in the midst of pain.

One reason I'm looking forward to heaven is that I'm tired of experiencing and seeing pain all around me—in a woman whose husband has repeatedly committed adultery, a friend killed in a car crash, a sixteen-year-old friend of my daughter who committed suicide, a friend who slowly died of emphysema, couples whose marriages are crumbling, people whose homes were destroyed by forest fires. I'm tired of miscommunicating with my wife. I'm tired of being barraged by blatant sexuality. I'm tired of back pain and tired of being tired.

Often God uses pain to teach us, non-Christians and Christians alike, about ourselves and to draw us toward himself. Even the strongest atheist or agnostic, the most confident businessperson or the most well-known and powerful community leader faces new territory when the new baby has a congenital heart defect, the spouse is critically injured in a car accident, the marriage falls apart or a brother gets AIDS. During such times of pain, many people recognize their need for God. How will we respond? Will the ways we show we care help a hurting person discover that God loves and cares?

Sometimes God gives us a special privilege to be present when people are hurting deeply. During those sacred moments, God uses us—our listening, our caring compassion—to touch the hearts of hurting people with his redemptive love.

JESUS DIDN'T HAVE ARTIFICIAL AGENDAS

Can you think of a time when Jesus used his relationship with a person superficially or manipulatively?

It didn't happen.

Jesus always dealt honestly with people. If he didn't agree with them, he said so. Or he said nothing. If they were turning the temple into a den of thieves, he drove them out. If he had the opportunity to confront corrupt religious leaders, he did so. When he met people, he cared about their deepest needs, not about whether he would be able to meet a quota for the day by telling X number of people about salvation.

RECOGNIZE DIVINE APPOINTMENTS

I believe God creates divine appointments for us. Patty learned this recently.

"Not long after Heather and her husband moved in across the street, I knocked on her door with some cookies to welcome her to the neighborhood. Heather opened the door and said, 'I don't want to meet anybody. I'm tired. I just got done unpacking, and you dragged me out of bed. And I don't want any cookies.' Then she slammed the door."

Patty began praying for Heather, reached out to her in small ways and invited her to come to a neighborhood book club. Heather accepted, and before long she and Patty were discussing spiritual things. Sometimes Patty's husband, Paul, joined in.

"When Heather discovered she was dying of cancer, she really let me into her life," Patty says. "She told me what she was struggling with and what she didn't like about God. She could even go back through her life and tell me about every Christian she had every encountered."

Heather's condition worsened. One night, after Heather went into a coma, her husband asked Paul if he'd come over and sit with her while the family did errands. "She hadn't been alert for several days," Paul said, "but as soon as I walked into the room she woke up, grabbed my hand and said, 'I want to talk with you about Christ.'" He explained the gospel and God's love for her for forty-five minutes. Then she lapsed back into the coma and died.

"God was faithful to Heather until the end," Patty says. "Paul and I are thankful that he used us during Heather's last months on earth. I delivered the eulogy at the funeral and was able to share Christ often, because her family and friends who came to our home after the funeral wanted to know why I'd done so much for someone I had only known for eighteen months."

The integrity of Jesus' life speaks to me, sometimes in ways I don't like. So I've had to ask myself questions such as these:

- When I speak with someone, do I try to steer the conversation to what I want to say, rather than really listening?
- Do I find myself talking about myself and what I know rather than exploring what the other person is thinking and feeling?
- When somebody seriously disagrees with me and makes me feel uncomfortable, do I strive to understand his or her position? Or do I allow myself to drift away to build an easier relationship with somebody else?
- Do I truly care about the needs of my neighbor, or are my motives mixed with efforts to win people's approval?
- Do I regularly pray for people I know who are not yet Christians and ask God to give me opportunities to connect with them?

BECOME AN EFFECTIVE LISTENER

Often Jesus used questions in his encounters and conversations. His question served various purposes:

- as a jumping-off point to teach truth (Mark 8:17-18)
- as a way to begin relationship (John 4:7)
- to honor people by inviting them to say what he could do for them (Matthew 20:32)
- to give people the opportunity to express their pain (Mark 9:21)
- to stimulate people's thinking (Luke 18:19)
- to focus on a needy person who needed special encouragement (Luke 8:45)
- to confront someone's insincere question (Luke 20:3)

You and I have tremendous opportunities to reflect Jesus' love to non-Christians by asking them sincere questions and listening carefully to their responses. Randy Raysbrook is excited about how we can use questions, and the curiosity they generate, to create interest in Jesus and the Bible's truth. "The goal of a good question," he remarked as we conversed one day, "is not just to get an answer; it is to provoke reflection. Often Jesus asked questions when he already knew their answers, but he used them to get people to reflect. What would happen if we let questions rule the day, not the answers? If we used questions to lead people down emergent paths toward Jesus—and delighted in their journeys? If need be, let's develop a collection of stimulating questions we can use to discover the personal stories of people who do not yet know Jesus."

Effective listening includes many benefits.

1. We can take advantage of natural opportunities to guide conversations toward spiritual topics.

2. Asking non-Christians appropriate questions—and really wanting to hear their answers—can open the door to learning a great deal about who they are, what they know about various subjects, and their beliefs and opinions. What better way than to give them the opportunity to talk and feel safe, without fear that we will attack them and back them into a corner? When asked the right questions sincerely, non-Christians often will reveal what they think about God, church, the nature of truth, capital punishment, Jesus. . . . In fact, if they know we care and it's safe to open up, they may divulge at a very vulnerable level—a painful situation at work, a child suffering from a car accident, a job setback, a breakup with a girlfriend or boyfriend, a pending divorce, fears.

3. Asking questions and listening to someone gives him or her honor. (It makes me feel good when someone chooses to listen to me, concentrating on what I say rather than doing or thinking about something else.) Everyone's story deserves to be heard.

4. Listening is a special way to express love. Often people need love more than just answers (although sometimes direct answers are essential). They want someone to care about them, to give them space

to reflect and wrestle with issues, to be there during the spiritual journey.

5. Asking questions engages people and reduces possible tensions. Instead of immediately arguing with a Christian who is "defending the faith," even hostile people can be brought into more cordial discussion when their forcefulness is deflected by calmly posed questions.

6. When we practice effective listening, we become more comfortable with non-Christians. False stereotypes break down. We begin to share more of ourselves, honestly and with passion, and our truthfulness and struggles resonate with non-Christians. They know that nobody has it all together all the time.

7. Sometimes God uses particular events in non-Christians' lives to give us opportunities to listen and build meaningful relationships.

About two weeks ago I visited Tony, a good friend who is, as I write this, experiencing some challenges. His father, who lives on the East Coast, has heart trouble and needs better care. Tony's year-long contract with his employer is also about to end, and he must decide whether to renew it. Since he has been commuting out of state for weeks at a time, there are also marital issues. His wife has handled his absence pretty well, but how would being gone three weeks out of every month affect their relationship during the course of another year?

I listened as he ran through the pros and cons of his job, and I asked deliberate questions I hoped would help clarify his thinking. As I did so, I became acutely aware of the great resources we have as Christians because of our relationship with God through Jesus. We can ask God for guidance, and he promises to provide it! We can ask him for wisdom. We can depend on him for what we need, and to give us the faith we need to keep on depending. And when the opportunities arise, we can share with non-Christians our stories of God's faithfulness and the relevance of biblical truth.

IT'S ABOUT US

Through the years, I have read books on evangelism and received training in "how to witness." Usually the emphasis is on content—points to raise, key verses to highlight, ways to introduce issues. *Witnessing* has been treated as a verb—something we *do* and then get back to daily life. Recently, though, Christians seem to be emphasizing *being a witness*. Here the emphasis is on who we *are*. Factors that deeply influence how we communicate and how well what we communicate is received are being explored. These factors include when to respond with questions, our vulnerability in sharing, tone of voice, nonverbal actions, timing and generating interest in spiritual things naturally.

It's becoming pretty clear that being a witness for Jesus involves much more than simply *doing witnessing* for a certain period of time. Being a witness involves everything we do and say in the course of everyday living, and love must be at the center of it all.

Love communicates. Practical demonstrations of love stand out in our sinful, self-centered world. People notice when we are filled with God's love; it overflows onto them!

Jeff certainly noticed, and his life completely changed.

Christians must be willing to listen as much as they speak if they ever hope to be heard and taken seriously. Listening communicates more respect than speaking (a very hard task when you are confident you possess the truth). Listening suggests we may actually have something to learn. Since we claim omniscience belongs to God alone and not ourselves, this shouldn't be a novel concept for Christians. . . . By listening we not only show respect, we also affirm truth in a friend's position, at which point we can point him or her to a greater, more comprehensive, more satisfying truth.

RICH NATHAN

JEFF'S STORY

Jeff was born into a middle-class family. His dad was in the U.S. Army, so the family moved a lot. His parents argued constantly, and they divorced when he was in his early teens.

At age thirteen, he began stealing beer and getting drunk. It took six weeks in a hospital to get his bleeding ulcer under control. He started skipping school and going to the beach. His mother remarried, which created new problems.

Then things got worse. His violent stepfather threatened to hurt Jeff. Sometimes the teenager cowered in his room holding a .22 rifle in case his stepfather broke down the door.

Not surprisingly, Jeff soon went to live with his father and his father's new wife in another state. Now a junior in high school, he partied heavily. After graduation, he sold encyclopedias door to door. When he wasn't working, he had sex with various women and became sexually addicted. "I did whatever felt good," he recalls. "It was a big party."

He joined the army, and there he found a few fellow soldiers who also enjoyed using LSD, cocaine and psychedelic mushrooms. Here's how Jeff describes what happened next:

> I wound up getting orders to go to Germany, and my friends gave me a going-away party complete with cocaine and a woman. I missed my plane and spent the next six months AWOL until I got arrested for selling cocaine. Because I had my military ID with me when they arrested me, the army couldn't charge me with desertion, so I was sent to a different army base to receive retraining.

Jeff continued to use and deal drugs and began partying with witches, warlocks and others involved in the occult who tried to recruit him.

> Somebody gave me a ritual about how to contact Satan and said, "If you do this, at this time, Satan will come and talk to you." That scared me to death, and I never told anyone else what the ritual was. I knew in my heart that the devil *would* come. He'd give me the food, sex, drink—all the pleasures I'd want, but the cost would be very high. I'd lose the ability to love. I knew it because that was already happening.

Satan was wooing Jeff—and hate was taking over. "I couldn't name five people I didn't hate," Jeff recalls. "Hate was eating me up from the inside." Five days after being reassigned to another base, Jeff went to his commanding officer and said, "Sir, I have to get out of the army. If you don't let me out, I'm going to kill somebody and end up in Leavenworth. I don't know who it might be. It could be you, the first sergeant, anybody in the barracks." Two days later Jeff was discharged.

Still dealing drugs, Jeff rented a house and hired an accountant to keep track of his drug money. But he couldn't stop thinking about his need to love instead of hate.

> I decided that I needed to love, so I started to give better deals on the drugs I sold. After a good friend ripped me off, I came close to having him killed, but I thought, *It's really not love to kill somebody, and I need to learn to love.* I still wanted to learn to love rather than hate. That's all I knew. I had removed myself from the military environment, but not from the drug environment. I knew my hatred came from Satan, so I tried to work on the antithesis to hate—love. But I didn't know how to do that. I kept trying to be loving on my own.

One evening Jeff met a woman named Gail, and the genuine love of God that overflowed from her touched him deeply.

> Gail had just become a Christian and started talking to me about Jesus. I had heard about him years earlier, but I hadn't heard that he loved *me*. That lit a spark. I was trying to love and not hate, but I really didn't know anything about love. Gail had a joy, a peace, a love I had never seen before. I talked with her several times; then she invited me to come to a little coffeehouse run by a small church. It was open seven nights a week, so lots of street people came. There I heard again that Jesus died for me and loved me. For seven nights in a row, I went to that coffeehouse.

Shortly after that, Jeff attended a Christian music concert at a church and received Christ. "Incredible things changed in my heart," he says. "I began to study Scripture and pray. God took away my hate and gave me the power to love. I often shared Jesus with street people."

THROW A BABY SHOWER

When a new couple moved into our neighborhood, I met them as they were fixing up their mailbox. Kristen was obviously pregnant, and after a few months my wife and another neighbor decided to throw a baby shower for her. They typed up invitations and delivered them to select neighbors. In addition to seeing the joy on Kristen's face during the shower, my wife met two women she didn't know.

Now a successful businessman, Jeff sums up his story this way:

God is awesome. Sometimes he allows us to go through some real hell and uses that hell to build us up, draw us close to himself. God wants me to love him, worship him, and walk with him in spirit and truth. He wants me to bring my hurt and pain to him and let him heal it. He wants me to take my hurt and pain and show others that no matter what any of us has done, God loves us. And we, in turn, can therefore love other people. I couldn't make love happen in my life, and I sure recognized it when I finally saw it—in Gail and the other Christians.

FOR REFLECTION AND DISCUSSION

1. Why is it important for us to share our *lives* with people, not just our words?

2. What kinds of people do you find it easy to love? What kinds are difficult to love? Why?

3. What does sacrificial love look like? What obstacles must we overcome in order to demonstrate this kind of love?

4. Where, ultimately, must our love come from? What happens if we try to generate it on our own?

5. Why do you think Gail's love stood out to Jeff?

6. Jesus said that people will know we are his disciples by our love. What happens when we substitute other things for love in order to demonstrate that we are followers of Jesus?

7. Why is it important for us to read passages like 1 Corinthians 13:4-8, 13?

8. What's the relationship between *feeling* love and *taking action* based on that love?

9. Which person(s) might God want you to lovingly connect with soon? What steps will you take to make yourself available to that person?

— 3 —

Learning to Receive and Give

Why is it so important to love God?

In part, because out of that relationship flows a genuine, heartfelt, sacrificial love for others.

Our lives become better now, not just in eternity.

Luis Palau

When I read the Gospels, I'm struck by the many different ways in which Jesus lovingly met people's needs. He didn't rely on one approach. When people wanted to discuss issues, he empathized with them—one on one or in small groups—and even met with them late at night. When people came to him for healing, he identified with their pain and healed them, often face to face. When thousands of them were hungry, he miraculously and compassionately gave them food. Why? "The Son of Man did not come to be served, but to serve, and to give his life as a ransom for many" (Matthew 20:28).

Jesus exchanged his heavenly status for earthly servanthood. He exchanged the glory of heaven for an impoverished life on earth (2 Corinthians 8:9), "taking the very nature of a servant, being made in human likeness. And being found in appearance as a man, he humbled himself and became obedient to death—even death on a cross!" (Philippians 2:7-8).

As a servant, Jesus constantly went out of his way to help people.

- He listened to the centurion's pleas, then healed his servant (Matthew 8:5-13).

- He prayed for young children (Matthew 19:13-15).

- He overheard two blind men crying out for him, stopped and healed them (Matthew 20:29-34).

- He heard Bartimaeus shouting for mercy, stopped, asked the blind man to come to him and healed him (Mark 10:46-52).

- His heart went out to the widow whose only son had died, and he returned life to the boy (Luke 7:11-15).

- He healed a man's shriveled hand in the synagogue (Luke 6:6-10).

- He carried on an intellectual discussion with Nicodemus in secret, as the religious leader apparently requested (John 3:1-21).

Jesus' life illustrates how important it is for us to meet people's needs—the needs *they* believe are important, not just the ones *we* think are important. And how important it is to allow people to meet our needs in return.

GOD USES OUR WEAKNESSES AND NEEDS

The older I get, the more aware I am of my weaknesses and needs. I am stiffer than I used to be when I get up in the morning. My eyes tire out more quickly when I read books or stare at a computer screen. I still don't know how to rebuild a carburetor on my truck when the accelerator pump quits working or fix the propane heater in the camper a friend just gave us. I'm not sure how to communicate effectively with my teenage daughter all the time, and rearing her seems like a big experiment in many ways.

On a deeper level, these and other weaknesses and needs remind me that a part of me doesn't like to admit I even have them. I want to be able to solve them, hide them away for another day or at least create the impression that I've got everything under control. But I can't.

After back surgery five years ago, I discovered how much of an in-

ASK FOR HELP

A few months ago I pulled out my chainsaw and couldn't get it to start. Not wanting to take it to a repair shop, I called a neighbor who is good with small engines and asked if he'd give me a hand. Half an hour later, tools in hand, he showed up and we took the saw apart. As parts dropped into a box, he and I talked about various things. When he left, my saw was running again and I had been able to express appreciation to a new friend.

ternal war I was fighting. There I was, having to teach my low-back muscles and discs how to work correctly so I could walk freely again, and I became terribly frustrated with all the things I couldn't do. I had gone from building a house, backpacking, hunting and skiing to circling the living room with a walker and being unable to tie my shoes. What was worse, I didn't want to admit that I needed help and tried to control things people did on my behalf. In short, I didn't want to be served by anyone.

God used that time to remind me of an obvious fact: as a part of the body of Christ, I need others in the body. But an equally important fact came to light during that time, one that still holds true today. When I ask non-Christians to help me in areas of weakness and need, God often uses those times to help me build bridges with them that can't be built easily in other ways.

During the last few years especially, God has often used my needs and weaknesses, and those of my family, to introduce us to non-Christians who have become great friends. In fact, I'm convinced that God works mightily when we ask for and receive help from people. Our non-Christian friends have taught my wife and me much about giving and receiving practical help motivated by love. God has clearly given many non-Christians a deep love for other people, and I can only think it's because he created them in his image.

I can't count the times God has used non-Christians' willingness to help us in order to give us opportunities to share Jesus' love and truth with them. In fact, their generosity and insights have helped us save money so we can continue in our full-time ministry of writing and editing Christian books. God has always met our financial needs, and quite often he has used non-Christians to do that by serving us. That isn't at all what I expected to happen when I first began building relationships outside Christian circles.

A friend of mine grew up in a Christian family. For reasons I do not yet know, he wants little to do with God. But if I have a problem with plumbing, the wood splitter or virtually anything else that needs to be fixed, he bends over backward (sometimes literally) to help me. One of my earliest memories of him is when he helped us to change a tire that went flat near his driveway. Our families exchange dinner invitations regularly, and I often drop over to visit them in the evening. I am the richer for knowing him and his wife, and the discussions we have are stimulating and enriching. He's the only friend I have who reads *Scientific American* the way I read *Reader's Digest*.

During a time when I had severe tendonitis in both wrists, another friend changed the oil in my car whenever I called him over a period of two years. He and I continue to meet for lunch occasionally, our families celebrate holidays together, and I recently was invited to attend his son's Eagle Scout ceremony.

When we were building our house and needed storage space, a guy we'd recently met invited us to store things in his old pottery shop. We took him up on his offer and are still in touch with him today. In fact, his son visited us recently, and I may join him and his father for a day of fishing sometime.

Later, when we were building an addition on our home, a new friend brought his backhoe and dug the long trench needed for the power lines. When I asked how much I owed him, he said, "A few dollars for diesel fuel."

Another time, when our computers wouldn't "talk" with each other and our printer, a non-Christian friend spent nearly a whole day troubleshooting until the system was working smoothly. This same guy helped us to complete a difficult concrete job in between our living room and library when we remodeled. Now, more than two years later, we take walks together, and he still invites us to call him anytime we need help with computers.

Two weeks ago a new friend spent hours loading my truck with firewood after I strained my back. He is the father of one of my daughter's friends, and we regularly take walks and see movies together. He and I have had a number of significant conversations concerning life, relationships, spiritual truth and rearing daughters.

One of our other neighbors came over and helped me fix my chainsaw, set up a virus protection program on my computer and cut trees. Now we take walks together regularly and discuss many topics. One of our last ones focused on morality and how it becomes established within a culture.

The father of another of our daughter's friends volunteered to repair my pickup truck's starter. He and I talked as I passed him wrenches, and we've remained in touch ever since. Not long ago he and his wife invited us to his home for a "great friends and family" high school graduation celebration. Another evening the four of us played a table game and talked for more than three hours.

I could go on and on, but you get the point. Why is asking non-Christians for help, or accepting it when they volunteer it, such an effective way to get to know them more deeply? As I think this question through, I come up with several reasons. First, most people like to use their skills and abilities to help others who are appreciative. They feel honored to be helpers, who have something of value to give. Second, non-Christians we meet are curious about my family and me—why we invite people over for dinner, what Christians are like, why we write Christian books. Third—and this one still surprises me (oh me of little faith)—a number of non-Christians who act as if they have everything together and have little or no need for God catch glimpses of God at work in our lives. I say "surprises" because I'm more and more aware of my sin and my failures and why I need God's grace and forgiveness. The fact that God uses me, a pretty basic clay vessel, amazes me.

CONNECTING THROUGH SERVING OTHERS

Just as God can bring non-Christians to serve us, he gives us opportunities to reach out to them. Every day, all around us, people just like us face great needs. Whether or not they are Christians, their children get involved with drugs or have other problems. They lose their jobs. Get lonely. Feel like failures. Can't sleep. Have marital problems. Get de-

CONFESS YOUR NEEDS

We all have strengths and weaknesses. One way of compensating for our weaknesses, and getting to know our neighbors better in the process, is to ask for help. Sometimes it's better to receive than to give!

I frequently begin projects without knowing how they will end. I experiment and learn as I go. This works well sometimes, but when I started to build a go-cart out of a cast-off riding lawnmower, I soon realized I was in over my head. So I invited a neighbor who was technically proficient to help me, and we had fun for four hours. During that time, he also shared several deep concerns.

Another time, when Amanda and I lived in a two-bedroom apartment, friends of ours from college days, Paul and Tina, arrived for a visit in an old car with worn-out brakes. I volunteered to help Paul replace them. We pulled off a wheel and began removing springs and other brake parts, but soon I knew we were in trouble. "Hey," I called out to a man walking by, "you know anything about brakes?"

He hesitated and then grinned. "A little bit." He passed along a few pointers and gave me his apartment number in the adjoining complex. That simple conversation developed into a relationship with him and his wife that lasted almost twenty-five years. And he became a Christian!

pressed. Have great material success but no sense of meaning and purpose. Get cancer. See friends die. Get in car accidents. Need someone to help them learn a skill. Make bad financial decisions.

Where there are needs, godly servants are needed.

Most of us remember the "deliberate acts of kindness" people do for us. Non-Christians do too. They appreciate it when we think of them with a phone call, card or practical help. When we are sensitive to their needs and respond in love, they notice! This isn't a formula. It is simply our conscious decision to help meet people's needs the way we'd like them to help us if we were in their shoes. Sometimes it requires great sacrifice. Other times it is easy to do.

Through the years I've met various Christians who have chosen to serve non-Christians sacrificially, to allow God's love and truth to overflow from their lives: overseas missionaries who endure great challenges and hardships, doctors and nurses working in an inner-city medical clinic in Chicago, families that live in Christian community among impoverished people, individuals who volunteer in soup kitchens and orphanages. Sometimes these sacrifices are high profile; usually they aren't.

Years ago I got a taste of the impact even simple acts of service can make, and this time God used my wife and me. We had purchased our first home in a quiet cul-de-sac. Directly across the street from us lived a couple who eventually separated. The mom was left alone with the kids and with home repairs to manage. When the house needed painting, we volunteered to help her and her two sons with the job. On the chosen Saturday, we showed up with brushes and sandpaper and got to work. By the end of the day, the house was repainted and we'd had plenty of time to talk. I felt good about what we'd accomplished, and deep inside I knew that God's love had flowed through us.

Years went by. One son graduated from a prestigious college and took a job at an activist organization dedicated to promoting diversity and challenging Christians and Christian influences in the local community. One day he heard a coworker vigorously condemn and ridicule Christians. He thought a moment, then said, "Not all Christians are like that.

Several of them helped my family paint our house." He told us that story years later.

We never can see the whole picture, but sometimes God allows us to see glimpses. We'll never know, at least here on earth, the full impact of our love. But I do hope that a few non-Christians will say of me, "Not all Christians are like that. I knew one who . . ." That's a testimony in the true sense of the word.

As I write this, I find myself asking several questions, and I invite you to think about them too. *What am I doing today to meet non-Christians' real needs? What do they see me doing because of the love of Jesus overflowing from me? Or am I so tied up with my agendas, deadlines and schedules that I don't spend much time creatively thinking how I can serve non-Christians in ways they will accept and appreciate?* I don't always like the answers to these questions, but I certainly don't want my faith to be a cold set of beliefs or doctrines. Sometimes, I confess, God almost has to force me out of my comfort zone in order to get me to serve others.

Not long ago, several good friends who live about a two-hour drive away dropped by for a late-afternoon visit. We hadn't seen them for a long time, so it was a delight to sit down with them. About fifteen minutes after they arrived, though, the phone rang. It was Paul, a guy I've known for years who has battled alcoholism. After several years of sobriety, he had jumped off the wagon. "Will you help me?" he asked. "I'm having nightmares. I need prayer bad." I directed him to call a local church that has an extensive counseling ministry. But when he called there, nobody answered the phone. So he called back ten minutes later. And then called a third time.

Finally I agreed to help Paul and rounded up other Christian men so we could all pray for him. After the prayer session, one of them and I accompanied Paul to his home and cleaned out all the empty and partially full cans and bottles left over from his binge drinking. Again we prayed for him, that God would deliver him. When I got home about 6:30 p.m., my out-of-town friends had gone home. I knew God had used me to make a difference in Paul's life, but I was also keenly reminded that serving others often has a price. Serving others is seldom easy or tidy.

Acts of service can be far more persuasive in guiding people toward Christ than mere words. In his book *Too Christian, Too Pagan*, Dick Staub emphasizes the importance of *showing* rather than preaching: "Aristotle said there are three components in persuasion: logic *(logos)*, passion *(pathos)*, and integrity *(ethos)*. He believed that all the logic and passion in the world would not persuade a person who could observe that your life didn't match your words."

Does my life have integrity with what I say I believe? That's my prayer. Am I perfect? No. But I want what I say I believe to be reflected in natural, sincere actions.

This past weekend, I led small group discussions in a prison in southern Colorado. As I spoke with inmates, I opened up about some things I struggle with, some mistakes I have made. I also talked about God's love and forgiveness. They listened and let down a few of their defenses too. I think they could tell that I genuinely cared about them—because I dedicated a weekend to be available to them inside the walls.

People will know that we are Christians by our love, and serving others demonstrates love that touches people at a deep level. Including those who seem to say nothing good about Christians, the Bible or the church. Including hardened prisoners who may spend the rest of their lives behind bars.

Everybody has needs, so helping to meet them is a great "bridge" that overcomes all kinds of personal and cultural differences. Many people hunger for meaningful relationships. If we genuinely love them, and our offer of help is a sincere byproduct of that love, they *know!*

Right now I visit a friend who recently had back surgery. It means a lot to him and his wife that I stop in for a little while every few days even though he lives about a twenty-minute drive away. When I missed several days and then stopped in, his wife said, "We wondered where you were and if you had forgotten us."

Do I remember the people who came by to talk with me after my back surgery, to lend me a video or book? You bet. And this guy was one of those people. I learned much about him as we talked for hours. In fact, I may be the only person to whom he has recounted the hell he experienced during the Korean and Vietnam wars.

Many non-Christians are hungry for the love and truth God provides, even if they don't yet realize it. Many are deeply appreciative when someone not only spends time with them but wants to get to know them and their particular needs.

One guy living near us doesn't have any equipment to move snow off his driveway. And since we live at 7,500 feet in Colorado, sometimes we get *lots* of the white stuff. For a while, when I had use of a tractor, I'd plow to the end of our long driveway, then drive down and plow out his

"ADOPT" LONELY PEOPLE

Holidays can be particularly difficult times for someone whose spouse has recently died or a college student who is unable to return home. Why not invite him or her over for a meal or a game night, or to watch a video and eat popcorn?

driveway. It only took a few moments, but it saved him and his wife hours of shoveling. Today both of them are becoming our friends, but a much greater investment of our time is needed.

Opportunities to help people pop up unexpectedly when we are sensitive to God's leading. One morning as I left a restaurant after a business meeting, I noticed a couple with two young children standing by a car with its hood up, so I walked over to see if I could help. As it turned out, they had just moved to Colorado and had no place to stay and no jobs.

I went back into the restaurant with them, found out their financial situation and the type of housing they were looking for, and arranged to call them later that day. Returning home, I called apartment complexes, selected a nice one in a good school district that would meet the family's budget and transportation requirements, and called the family back with the address and person to contact. The family moved in shortly afterward, thankful that a virtual stranger had helped them. And I was blessed to have had the chance.

Occasionally I interact with wealthy people who drive luxury cars, hold lavish parties, live in huge houses, vacation in exotic spots and—to be honest—intimidate me sometimes. *They seem so satisfied with life,* I find myself thinking. *Even without God, they seem happier and friendlier than some Christians I know. What can I possibly do for them?*

Yet these men and women face the same, or even greater, struggles. Many compete in challenging career environments in which they sink or swim. They often manage employees, so they experience the strains of cash flow, benefit plans and the like. Some of them have achieved everything they wanted in life, but inside they aren't fulfilled. Another car, another vacation, another award just doesn't cut it or bring the pleasure it once did. They also face marital challenges, want to be better fathers and mothers, and deal with family crises. They have flat tires, experience panic when a child wanders away during a picnic or—as happened in various U.S. states last summer—have to flee their homes when wildfires burn out of control. So they also need people who will care about them, reach out with practical help and won't impose hidden agendas on them.

> *If anyone has material possessions and sees his brother in need but has no pity on him, how can the love of God be in him?*
>
> 1 JOHN 3:17

You know what broke down walls initially between us and a non-Christian single guy? He invited me to attend a party for ski club friends. And he did that knowing (1) I never was a good skier and may never be able to downhill ski again because of my back surgery, (2) I wouldn't know anybody at the party, and (3) he hardly knew me.

I decided to go and try to serve, or at least stay out of the way and be present. And I found my niche—cooking on his barbecue grill and serving meat! All I had to do was go around and ask, "Who's ready for a burger? How 'bout some chicken? I got hot dogs," for two hours.

Things went so well that he invited me back the next day, to a party for a different group of friends! (I guess he figured, when you're single and get the house cleaned, why not get all the mileage out of that you can?) I cooked much of the meat then too. The result? He and I became great friends, and I regularly connect with him. He hasn't shown much affinity for anything spiritual yet, but I'll keep praying.

> When I know their [non-Christians'] hearts, I can begin to speak their language. I'm aware of where my interests and experiences overlap with theirs, and that helps me speak biblical truth with grace and understanding. . . .
> At the same time, . . . they start seeing us as real persons with real struggles, but with a faith big enough to provide real answers in the midst of real challenges.
>
> **DAVID HENDERSON**

Chances are you already know someone who is needy. Someone whose husband or wife is ill. A single parent struggling to raise a teenager. A twentysomething person who just can't seem to figure out a career path or is getting divorced after a year or two of marriage. Someone whose money never stretches to the next payday. Someone who struggles to stop drinking. A lonely person who just doesn't fit in. A young man or woman trapped in sexual sin. Someone who can't do necessary yardwork due to an injury. A widow or widower who appreciates regular "touch-base" phone calls. Someone whose child is in the hospital. A professor, openly critical of Jesus, who carries around burdens of guilt she cannot shrug off. The list could go on. If you faced a similar situation, what would you like someone to do for you? What can you do to help?

If you don't know a needy person, ask your pastor or a community leader to link you up with someone to whom you can show Jesus' love. Perhaps you could drive someone to a chemotherapy treatment. Or tutor a child who needs help in mathematics or reading. Or come alongside a stressed-out single parent. Or take a meal to a family whose mother is ill.

Or loan videos to someone who is bedridden after surgery.

The following story, told to me by Cory Hardesty, illustrates how God can use our helpfulness in significant ways—ways we may never discover until we get to heaven!

When I was young, my mother received Christ and began taking us to church. But my father was playing in golf tournaments every Sunday and wouldn't come with us. Still, my six-year-old brother kept inviting him. One day my brother said, "Daddy, you say you'll go to church with me. Will you please go with me today?"

So my father went, and he said to my mother, "If anybody touches me or messes with me, I'm out of there." As he sat in the back pew with my mother, he saw one of his former drinking buddies in the choir. At the end of that service, my father was deeply moved by the love of God and received Christ a few weeks later. He quit the bar scene and joined the church softball team.

One day he hurt his back while playing first base during a church league game, and we took him home. There he was, lying on the couch, with two young children, and we were supposed to be moving into another house we'd just bought. So Christians from the softball team came over to help my family pack things up and move in.

My dad had planned to remodel the kitchen and the bathroom in our new home and repaint everything in stages when we had enough money. But now he couldn't. Meanwhile, two contractors from the church talked to one another during a prayer time and knew that God wanted them to remodel our home. So they offered their services. My dad said, "Thanks, but we don't have the money to do that right now."

"I don't think you understand what I'm telling you," one replied. "I'm going to remodel your home for free. All you have to do is pay for some of the materials."

My grandfather came by one day and watched the remodeling.

Grandpa was a professional fighter—tough, self-sufficient and a hard worker. He never went to church and believed that church people had absolutely nothing he wanted. He loved us children, had a great heart, was successful in his business. But when he drank, he became verbally abusive.

When he visited, my grandfather remarked to my dad, "Wow, this is something, but this has to cost some real money."

"No, Dad, I'm not paying for most of it," my dad replied. "God told them to do this for us, and they are doing it." Several people from the church who owned a paint store later painted our house for free.

My grandpa couldn't believe it and returned several times to watch the two guys spending all this time away from their families to remodel our house for several weeks. It was the first time he'd ever seen love demonstrated like this. *How can anyone love my son with a love like this?* he wondered. *I've never had that kind of love. Why are they doing this?* Within a short time, wanting what those Christians and my father had, my grandfather received Christ.

Not long after that, my father took a new job out of state, so we really weren't able to enjoy the benefits of the remodeling work for long. But God knew that the remodel wasn't for my parents; it was for my grandpa, for whom we'd been praying. And nobody besides God, not even the contractors, knew that.

God softened my grandfather's hard, cold, tough exterior. He became a college coach in Idaho and reflected Christ to many people.

Several years ago an article in a Christian magazine challenged readers to invite one non-Christian over for dinner once a month. If each of us did this, think how many people we'd meet, how many people could be exposed to the love of Christ and how much we'd learn from people who think quite differently from us.

A number of churches are becoming aware of how important it is for Christians to reach out to their communities in practical, caring

WATCH SOMEONE'S HOUSE

If you learn that a neighbor will be out of town for an extended period of time, offer to mow the lawn, collect the mail or help in other ways. We've been sharing Jesus' love in this way with one family for years, and it's amazing how much it means to them when we take care of their cats and water their flowers.

ways. So they offer free car washes, hand out free soft drinks at sporting events, assist at soup kitchens, distribute turkey dinners, help senior citizens with small repair projects and run food pantries for needy families. A church in New York City handed out water to people streaming past their doors right after the 9/11 attacks on the World Trade Center.

Paul wrote to the Thessalonians: "We continually remember before our God and Father your work produced by faith, your labor prompted by love, and your endurance inspired by hope in our Lord Jesus Christ" (1 Thessalonians 1:3). I don't know about you, but I'd love for someone to remember me with words like these someday at my memorial service.

FOR REFLECTION AND DISCUSSION

1. What are some reasons people hold back from helping others or from asking for help?

2. Do you agree that helping to meet someone's needs can be an effective way of getting to know him or her? Why or why not?

3. What needs do you have that a non-Christian might be able to help you meet? What might keep you from asking him or her for help?

4. Which particular skill(s) do you have that you might be able to use to help someone?

5. Think about non-Christians you know and what you know about them. Which of them have needs? How might you be able to come alongside and help meet someone's need this coming week? (Pickup

truck? Rototiller? Books? Extra car? Spare bedroom? A gift certificate
for a meal out or free babysitting?)

6. Think about times when people have helped you. What made those
   times special for you and the other person?

7. Which point(s) stood out to you as you read this chapter? Why?

8. Why is it so important for our actions to match our words? What
   happens if they don't? In what ways has Christians' lack of integrity
   between words and actions hurt the cause of Christ?

Using Our Opportunities Wisely

People around us are on a spiritual journey.

They are like blind men trying to find their way.

Sometimes their agony is so great, it is as if they are crying out for mercy.

God is at work in their lives directing them into our path.

DICK STAUB

One day I went to my dentist for a routine tooth cleaning. Sensitive and caring, he had once left a golf course to help me when one of my teeth cracked as I ate a pecan roll. Now here I was again, sitting in his dental chair with my head tilted back and a bright light shining in my eyes. Dr. R. bent over me with a mask over his mouth, peering at my teeth through magnifying lenses. And of course *the machine* was going. You know, the one that goes *SssPfftSss* as the tube dangling from your mouth seems as if it is trying to remove all liquid from your body, not just your mouth. As I tried to envision myself being anywhere but in that chair, I had the distinct impression that God wanted me to share Jesus with Dr. R. during my dental visit.

No, that can't be right, I thought. *Here I am in this silly chair, with my mouth open and this plastic tube in it, and I'm supposed to share Jesus?* So I didn't say anything of substance during the rest of my dental examination, even after the "saliva sucker" had been removed.

Early that next week, I read in the local newspaper that Dr. R. had died while swimming at a health club.

It's painful to tell this story, but it reminds me of the importance of listening to the Holy Spirit's voice and doing what God wants me to do even if it seems awkward, stupid or even a bit aggressive. He wants us to be sensitive enough to his leading to take advantage of the opportunities he gives us, even if they seem strange.

Opportunities to Love

Sixteen-year-old Al spoke loudly and intimidated people. Just under six feet tall and muscled, he often regaled male seatmates on the school bus with turn-my-cheeks-beet-red tales of his sexual exploits. Then he bought a souped-up car and quit riding the bus. I was, to be honest, a bit relieved.

Peter, an avid hunter and fisherman, let me use his pickup truck to haul away trash. His divorce was nearing, and I didn't know what I could say to him that would make any difference. Besides, he was quite suspicious of anybody "religious." So I kept things on a polite-conversation level.

Susan claimed to have been a Christian once. When I met her, she and her husband rode large motorcycles and made it a point to emphasize that they didn't need what Christianity had to offer. When they quit returning our phone calls, I let time create distance and put relational energy into other people.

Ralph, a neighbor, made it clear to me that he had a drinking problem and didn't like neighbors much. After accidentally offending him, I thought it'd be best to just leave him alone. So I didn't apologize and did just that. *He's too hardened against people to try to befriend,* I rationalized.

What do these people have in common? They are but a few of the people who come to mind when I think of opportunities I've missed to reflect Jesus. I never took the opportunity to find out what these people are really like—their hopes and dreams, their pain, their goals—due to my stereotypes of them and misplaced priorities. I also allowed things to hinder my ability to hear the Holy Spirit—being too busy and self-centered, not dealing with my sins appropriately, feeding my mind with many things but not enough of the Bible, not realizing how much God wanted to use me to share his love and truth in everyday life.

The closer I walk with God, though, the more sensitive I am becoming to his guidance and discernment. Obviously he doesn't want me to play a key role in the life of every non-Christian I meet. Each of us is limited by timing, location, temperament, interests and so on. God seems to open relational doors naturally rather than forcing them open, just as he allows us to choose whether or not we will open our hearts to him.

There's another side to God's timing. Sometimes he releases us from involvement with non-Christians. For example, he enabled me to reach out to a person who moved away a few months later. In another instance, I was able to begin the process of discipling someone, and then God brought another Christian into my friend's life who is picking up where I left off. Sometimes, to use Jesus' agrarian model, I am a cultivator. Other times I'm a planter, a waterer or a harvester. And sometimes I'm just not supposed to have any particular role in someone's life.

Just as a number of Christians have influenced my spiritual life in significant ways, God often brings a number of people into a non-Christian's life during his or her spiritual journey. Think for a moment about how many people God used to bring you to himself. It may be quite a long list!

We never know how God may use our seemingly insignificant comments or expressions of love, or those of someone else. One young woman made a huge impact on my life years ago, and she never even knew it. An agnostic in my early twenties, I went on a weekend camping trip with Christian friends from college. The morning after we arrived at the campground, a Sunday, my friends decided to stand around the fire and sing Christian songs. My heart and mind ached, and I walked away. *I can't sing songs like that,* I thought sadly, *but I wish I could.* After years of

INVITE A FRIEND

Carol Mayberry, who has three children and a busy husband, doesn't have much free time. So she has this philosophy about using and creating opportunities to share with non-Christians: "I do things I like to do recreationally, or as a hobby, or as a work project—and invite other people to participate. An example is the book club a friend and I started eight years ago. And if I want to go to a women's film festival or on a hike, I try to think of people to call up and invite." Which people might you invite to do something you enjoy?

Some of the greatest conversations I've had with non-Christians have taken place while hiking, driving home from a hunting trip, cross-country skiing and after meals in our home.

If you are a mountain-bike aficionado and you notice that a neighbor has a bike, why not suggest a time to ride a trail together? If you enjoy taking your family to the pool, invite neighbors to tag along. Perhaps the local library is starting a new film series. Or your church has put together a special drama presentation. Or you have been given free tickets to a downtown event. Quite often people will feel honored to be invited. Even if they can't come, the invitation will mean a great deal and communicate your interest in the relationship.

debate and struggles with the Christian faith, I earnestly desired peace and joy. *I wish I weren't so tied up in knots, so anguished in mind,* I thought, walking farther away.

"Hey Stephen," a woman I didn't know well called out, "please come back and join us. You don't have to sing—just be with us."

When I turned around, her wonderful smile, full of love, penetrated my layers of philosophical argument and emotional pain. It cut through to the deepest part of me, and I walked back to the group a spiritually changing person.

My intellectual questions remained, and many challenges still lay ahead of me. But the love of God expressed through that smile broke down my defenses and jump-started my spiritual journey toward him.

My prayer now is that God will make me especially sensitive to situations in which he wants me to respond to people in a particular way. Maybe it's with a smile, a word of encouragement or a long-term commitment of relationship. Maybe it's with a simple, two-minute story of how God and the Bible have helped me during a difficult situation.

Paul wrote, "Be very careful, then, how you live—not as unwise but as wise, making the most of every opportunity. . . . Be wise in the way you act toward outsiders; make the most of every opportunity" (Ephesians 5:15-16; Colossians 4:5). Our responses have eternal consequences.

Several hours before I began working again on this chapter, I met a twenty-three-year-old man for breakfast. He works at a health club where I work out, and from the beginning, as soon as I showed sincere interest in him, he began confiding deeply personal things to me. To open the "door" further, I mentioned that I'd enjoy having breakfast or lunch with him sometime, and earlier this week he approached me and asked if today would work. As I discovered, most of his life has been very difficult—his mother has died, his father is imprisoned, he has experienced cruel relatives, abuse, foster homes. But still he has a wonderful tenderness about him and has clung to his dreams. My wife and I plan to invite him and his girlfriend over for a meal before long. He needs to experience the deep love of God that has transformed my view of myself.

What does God want to do in and through me as a result of this contact? I don't know, but I'm sure God will guide me—one step, one conversation, one meal at a time. And if my new friend moves away in several months, as he may do in order to attend college, perhaps we'll exchange letters. Or God will lead me to pray regularly for him, specifically that he will meet another Christian with whom he can open his heart.

GOD'S PERFECT TIMING

Sometimes God's direction is so obvious that we cannot avoid it, as I discovered during what I thought would be an uneventful airplane ride.

I arrived at the Colorado Springs airport at 5:30 one morning to catch a flight to California. Trying to wake up, but not being a coffee drinker, I started to read a newspaper. But my eyes were too tired to read, so I looked around and studied people. My eyes were quickly drawn to a scene unfolding across the lobby. A woman was arguing with a flight attendant about luggage. Back and forth they volleyed, voices rising.

My oh my, I thought. *I sure wouldn't want to sit next to that woman. It's not even 6:00, and already she's arguing!*

Well, about ten minutes later you know what happened: I found myself seated next to that woman. I must admit that I wasn't thinking about showing her Jesus' love. In fact, I thought about moving to a different seat. Clearly I had to make a split-second decision. I could go back to the reading rack and get a golfing magazine, even though I have never picked up a golf club. I could pretend to sleep and end up with a crick in my neck. I could just sit there and hope she didn't notice me.

Suddenly she blurted out a complaint about the flight attendant's insensitivity. "I recently had back surgery," she said, "and I'm not supposed to lift anything heavier than a soup can. And she wouldn't even carry my little bag onto the plane."

About this time I decided to try to make the best of the situation. As she told me about the car accident she had been in, I listened. She told me how disoriented she had been ever since and how hard it had been to concentrate in her work as a mortgage broker. "I've been to the doctor," she told me, "but he doesn't know what's wrong with me. I'm tired all the time. I can't make decisions well. I'm irritable, and it takes everything I have just to cope with the smallest stresses. My husband says I'm like a different person."

I realized she was describing how I'd felt for a year after a hit-and-run driver smashed into my car going sixty miles an hour. My car completely spun around several times, slid more than one hundred feet and was totaled.

I had to make another decision. Would I keep nodding and say as little as possible, or let down my defenses and tell part of my story?

Fortunately I decided to take a risk and let her know that I understood a little about what she was going through. I told her about my back pain and how, during the crash, my brain had been bruised, which had led to symptoms similar to those she was describing. I told her about soft-tissue damage to my muscles and ligaments, how irritable and restless I'd been, and how my wife had wondered if I'd ever get better.

The woman started firing questions at me. Hope began to replace despair as she realized that I understood her situation.

Before our plane landed, I talked a bit about how God had helped my wife and me face the pain resulting from my accident and keep our marriage together.

Then it happened. As the plane taxied to a stop, she turned to me with a big smile and asked, "Are you an angel?"

Knowing that I didn't have any wings under my T-shirt that day, I said, "No. Why do you ask?"

"Well, why did I sit next to you, of all people, on this flight? And why do you understand how I feel when even the doctor can't figure things out and my husband doesn't know what to do with me? And the brain-bruise symptoms you described are exactly like mine!"

Every day you and I meet people. Some of them we'll see again. Others, like that woman, appear only briefly in our lives. I'm glad I shared a bit of my personal story with her. (And it is probably the only time anybody will ever compare me to an angel, as my wife, daughter and friends will attest.)

But you know, I don't always take risks to let others know what God has done for me. In fact, sometimes I do everything I can to avoid them and keep my story (and God's story) to myself.

Can you relate?

Recounting the discussion on that plane reminded me of several things. First, I need to be careful when I make assumptions about people in an airport lobby—or anyplace—before 6:00 in the morning. Actually, it's best for me to allow God to guide me to the people he wants me to meet, whether or not I'm aware of my assumptions. Second, when I am willing to participate in the process, God will use parts of my story (even painful ones) in unusual ways. That woman never heard the rest of my story. She didn't need to. God placed me next to her so I could say a few words that brought hope to her suffering heart and mind.

> The United States has so many unchurched people that Christians living in other countries are sending missionaries here and consider this nation to be a primary missions target.
>
> GLENN PAAUW,
> INTERNATIONAL BIBLE
> SOCIETY

Today you may meet someone on a bus, in class, at work or in your neighborhood who needs to hear part of your story.

Every day we must choose whether or not we will connect with non-Christians. When we see a neighbor planting flowers, we can stop to talk or walk on. We can talk with the woman in the corner grocery store or hurry home. We can sit down next to a new coworker in the company cafeteria or sit with a friend from church. We can tug someone's car out of the ditch with our four-wheel-drive or keep going so we can be home in time for dinner. We can cook a meal for a family or not. We can help someone fix a tractor or complete our own chores.

A MEANINGFUL CONNECTION

Sometimes I think God laughs as his plans work themselves out—plans we can hardly fathom—when we manage to listen to his still, small voice and share his love and truth with people within our circles of influence.

About three years ago I decided to buy a used pickup truck. I determined the features it needed: large engine for pulling heavy loads, four-wheel-drive, four-speed transmission with a "granny low," extended cab and full-size bed. I told a friend who owns an auto body shop about this, and he replied, "Good luck in finding one. Lots of people want a truck like that, but I'll keep my eyes open."

A week later he called me and said, "I found your truck." Parked a few miles from our home with a for-sale sign on it, the truck turned out to be perfect. So I bought it from a guy I'll call Carl.

Carl was a pilot who worked unusual hours, so it was several days before he and I could meet to get an emissions inspection on the truck and handle the title transfer. We met at a predetermined location, and I invited him to ride with me to the bank. Upon arrival, Carl discovered he'd left his title in the truck, so back we went, talking all the while. Then we drove back to the bank. The more we talked, the more I realized that maybe this was one of those "God-ordained" conversations.

Carl's marriage was in trouble because he was sexually addicted, and his job gave him plenty of opportunities to live out his fantasies with flight attendants. But he did love his wife, he said, and wanted to get his

WELCOME NEIGHBORS WARMLY

In our semirural neighborhood, there are three easy signs that someone new has moved in:

1. a moving van or collection of loaded pickup trucks

2. a once-vacant house that is now occupied

3. a new child at the bus stop

Study your neighborhood for signs like these. When somebody new moves in, demonstrate Christian hospitality. Stop by with cookies. Pass along information on where to buy certain items or the best hair salon or automobile repair shop. Answer questions about local activities. Offer to help in any way possible. What a difference a smile can make! Hospitality is emphasized throughout Scripture, and it's a great way to break down barriers and demonstrate Christ's love.

life under control. I invited him to have breakfast with me. Several weeks later we talked at length about his marriage, sexual addiction, job and God. Not long after that, my wife and I invited Carl and his wife to come over for a picnic. They accepted, and we had hours of pleasant conversation. Before they left, I lent him a Christian book on dealing with sexual addiction (*False Intimacy* by Harry Schaumburg).

During the next year, I periodically left messages on his answering machine. Then a package arrived, along with a letter from his wife. They had separated. She wrote:

> Enclosed please find the book you loaned [Carl] several years ago. . . . I'd also like to thank you for your kindness to [Carl] during a particularly difficult period. I know he was grateful for your friendship and conversations and, due to the shortness and infrequency of contact, it might have seemed insignificant to you, but it was meaningful to him and came at a time when he was searching. You were one of many doors God opened for him during those years, and I know he always thinks of you with great warmth and appreciation. He . . . seems just recently to finally be making real progress in finding his faith and solidifying his character and life.

I wrote back to her, sent her a New Testament devotional product and received a nice note back. God had given me the opportunity to plant spiritual seeds and do a bit of watering. The rest is in his hands—where it has really been all along anyway.

Was it an accident that I decided to buy Carl's pickup? I don't think so. God uses all kinds of situations to give us opportunities to share his love and truth. Think of the people you meet during the summer, when your car breaks down, when your teenager brings friends home or when there's a disaster in your community. This morning I received a call from Mormon friends inviting me to come watch them putting up foods for long-term storage. I drove over and discovered the canning was finished, but I still had a delightful visit with the couple while they stained their deck.

THE FLU INCIDENT

Sometimes God uses sickness in his plan. A friend arrived at our home for a night's stay and became ill after my wife left to run a few important errands.

Giving someone a cup of chicken soup and a thermometer isn't all that hard to do. You sneak in, announce the soup is ready to drink, lay the thermometer on a table and duck out quickly. But as flu will sometimes do, this particular strain caused a "reverse-gravity situation" from the stomach. Before I knew it, I was holding a pan in front of our friend's face.

Building a relational bridge to another person isn't very difficult, especially when you know the key: listening to the other person. . . . It's asking him questions. It's finding out about his world.

LEE STROBEL

I didn't think too much about it until she said later, "Thanks for helping me. Nobody has ever helped me like that before. My ex-husbands just left me alone when I got sick."

Today she stops by our home several times a year. She attends Church of Religious Science services and has not yet decided to follow Christ. But I know of at least one time when his love got through to her—through a metal mixing bowl.

SENSITIVITY TO THE FATHER'S WILL

Jesus personified what it means to walk with God and to pursue his Father's will. During his public ministry, he was always sensitive to what his Father wanted him to do and used every opportunity to share love and truth with people, even when it was inconvenient.

Doing the will of his Father was so important to Jesus that he compared it to the physical food people need in order to stay alive: "My food . . . is to do the will of him who sent me and to finish his work" (John 4:34). He remained dedicated to doing the Father's will even when it meant going to the cross for the sins of humanity (Mark 14:32-36). Jesus

WATCH FOR SPECIAL OPPORTUNITIES

Opportunities to meet others' needs aren't always obvious. Occasionally we have to initiate the action, not merely respond to a situation. One snowy morning at the bus stop, having dropped my daughter off, I noticed a woman I'd never seen before. So I introduced myself.

"We just moved here," she volunteered, "and we're trying to move in. But the moving company won't deliver our things until we get the driveway plowed." Fourteen inches of snow had fallen the night before. "Do you know anyone who can plow it by eleven o'clock? The moving company wants to come today."

Knowing that the professional snowplowers were fulfilling contractual commitments, I shook my head. Then I realized that maybe God wanted me to help her. I borrowed another neighbor's tractor and plowed her driveway and a path to her back stairs. That led to various discussions with her and her husband, who invited us to their home for a meal. The head of a multinational company in Korea, she has never forgotten that Christians she had never met plowed her out for free.

also sternly reminded others of the eternal consequences of doing or not doing God's will: "Not everyone who says to me, 'Lord, Lord,' will enter the kingdom of heaven, but only he who does the will of my Father who is in heaven" (Matthew 7:21).

As we seek to obey God and do his will, the Holy Spirit guides us. Sometimes he prompts us to pray. Sometimes he directs us away from dangerous situations. Sometimes he leads us to share his truth with people in unexpected ways. Let me give you another example.

During a flight from Chicago to Denver, I sat across the aisle from a guy who appeared to have it all together. The tailored suit he wore cost more than most of the clothes I own combined! In between confident statements about his executive position in an international company, he read a book about parenting. I felt that God wanted me to say something about the book, so I asked a general question. He replied curtly that it was written by a Mormon and contained helpful information.

I know a polite turnoff when I hear one, so I didn't pursue the subject after that except to say, "You know, my wife and I developed a New Testament-related book that has helped people look at what God says about lots of things, including family. Sometimes I send a copy to people I meet during my travels."

Then I shut up. *Okay, God,* I prayed silently, *I'm not going to offer to send him a copy. If you want him to have a copy, make it really clear to me. Otherwise I'll assume I've done what you wanted me to do.*

The airplane landed half an hour later in Denver, and my family met me not far from the gate area. (This was prior to the events of 9/11.) We walked quite a distance, went down an escalator and waited for a shuttle that would take us to another terminal building. Suddenly the man with whom I had spoken ran up to me. Panting, he handed me his business card, on which he had written his home address.

"Would you please send me that book you mentioned?" he asked.

"You bet," I answered. I sent him a copy the next day, and he e-mailed me a thank-you note.

God wants to use you in his unfolding plan to connect with people in your home, neighborhood, workplace, school. Wherever you go, he will guide you to the right people, whether they are in buses, trains, subways, airplanes or their front yards.

George Müller, a nineteenth-century social worker who sought to depend fully on God, had many opportunities to share Jesus' love and truth. The following observations he made in 1856 remain relevant to us today:

> The disciples of the Lord Jesus should labour with all their might
> in the work of God as if everything depended on their exertions;
> and yet, having done so, they should not in the least trust in their
> labour and efforts, and in the means which they use for the spread
> of the truth, but in God; and they should with all earnestness seek

the blessing of God, in persevering, patient, and believing prayer.

Here is the great secret of success, my Christian reader. Work with all your might; but trust not in the least in your work. Pray with all your might for the blessing of God; but work, at the same time, with all diligence, with all patience, with all perseverance. Pray then, and work. Work and pray. And still again pray, and then work. And so on all the days of your life. The result will surely be abundant blessing. Whether you *see* much fruit or little fruit; *such* kind of service will be blessed.

God, who is at work all around us, uses even the smallest opportunities to reveal his presence and power. We don't always *see* his work, but we can know it's happening.

Jesus said to grumbling Jews, "No one can come to me unless the Father who sent me draws him" (John 6:44). If we are open to what God wants to do in and through us, we're right where we need to be. I have walked right by opportunities God set up for me to tell the story of what God has done in my life. I will probably miss a number of future opportunities as well. But I don't want to miss out on what God wants to teach me through my spiritual journey. I don't want to miss out on how he wants to use me in someone else's life, either.

KRISTINE'S STORY

I met Kristine through a mutual friend. The following story, in her own words, illustrates the opportunities God gives us when we are sensitive to his leading and the joy we feel when we see him use us in someone's life.

I'm a nurse, and a few years ago I decided to take a three-month refresher course in nursing so I could sharpen my skills and have options to work in several different places. During the course, I met Lori, who had graduated from nursing school but had not yet passed her final board certification examinations.

We developed a friendship. Lori was married, in her early twenties, and had a little girl named Karen. The more I got to know Lori, the more I highly respected her. She had clear goals and direction, but many needs. Her relationship with her husband was rather strained. He was unhappy and not finding satisfaction in his job.

I tried to take the initiative by inviting her to have coffee with me. She wasn't used to having somebody reach out to her, and I tried to make comments that would flow naturally about God's importance in my life, what he meant to me. But I didn't say too much. We also talked in breaks when we had clinicals on the same floor in a hospital. I prayed for her regularly, feeling like the Lord was laying her on my heart.

Lori hadn't grown up in a church and was unfamiliar with Christianese. So I mostly tried to live my faith, to live the love and concern for her. She'd listen and wasn't offended, but wasn't drawn to it either. After we graduated from the class, we kept in touch by phone once every two or three months.

Kristine got a job working in the same hospital in which Lori worked. Sometimes they worked together, and Kristine felt as if the Lord was keeping them connected. Then she had to change occupations for health reasons and lost touch with Lori for a while.

After moving into a new house, Lori invited Kristine to visit. She was pregnant again, working twelve-hour shifts, hardly seeing her husband and busy caring for her high-strung daughter. But she was determined to be successful and leery of asking anybody for favors.

When Kristine went over to the house, Lori's daughter was starved for attention. So Kristine took time to play ball with her, read to her and give her undivided attention. As Kristine was leaving, Lori said, "Thank you so much for playing with Karen. It means a lot to me that you'd take that much interest in her."

About six months after the baby was born, Lori called and asked Kristine for help. A relative was dying in another state, and she and her husband needed to visit him. So Kristine took Lori's children into her house.

It wasn't easy. The baby didn't sleep all night and was ill, and I certainly wasn't used to being up all night and all day. But because I was willing to take care of her kids and put my schedule aside, my relationship with Lori became much closer and I could share more. "I have no idea how you work full-time and raise these children," I said. "I'm really praying that God will give you the strength to do what you need to do. And at the same time, you need to be wise and careful and take care of yourself." I tried to walk that fine line between being like her mother and being a friend.

We started talking on the phone for long periods of time, and she shared things with me that she'd never shared with anyone else. She realized she could trust me. I did a lot of listening—and didn't say much about God.

Then came September 11, and Lori became very fearful. I felt God saying to me, "It's time to tell her specifically about me. It's time to give her some hope, some answers."

I invited her out to lunch, and as we talked she suddenly said, "You know, I was lying in bed last night and said to my husband, 'What if they bomb our house, or our city? What will happen to us when we die?' My husband said, 'We're good people, Lori, so don't worry about it. We're going to heaven. We haven't killed anybody or robbed any banks.'" She then asked me, "What do you think?"

That open-ended question gave me the opportunity to share what I thought, and then I asked her, "Lori, have you ever gone to church?"

"Well," she replied, "I remember my dad took me once, and I had to learn a verse."

"What was that verse?"

Lori then recited John 3:16 perfectly and said, "That's the only thing I remember about church. I don't know what that means and what God is saying in that." So we looked at it closely, several words at a time, and she was amazed. Then I explained to her how she could invite Christ into her life and have a personal relationship with him, and that he loved her. "Are you ready for that?" I

OPEN YOUR HOME

Is your coworker's son or daughter getting married in a few weeks, in the company of many out-of-town guests? Will friends and neighbors be arriving for the funeral of one of your neighbors? If you have an extra bedroom, why not offer it for a single or family? You don't have to put on a production; be yourself and be helpful. Such hospitality touches people deeply, and it's unusual in this day when home for many people is viewed as a fortress, a place to hide after a long day, rather than a place in which to demonstrate love and hospitality.

asked. "Is that something you want to do?"

"Oh yes," she said. God had prepared her heart.

I told her that God wanted to come in and intervene in every area of her life, that he cared about her future and character development and all of that.

She prayed to receive Christ right there in the restaurant. I gave her some materials because I had felt God leading me to bring them. I gave her a Bible (she'd never had one), some devotional materials and a book to help her explore the book of John. Then I said, "Lori, I'd like to be available to help you walk through this process and learn what the Bible is all about and what this relationship really means."

Since then I've met with her various times. It's important that I show her that just because she has become a Christian our relationship isn't over. Now I can say to her, "I'm praying for you," and she responds warmly and appreciates it.

It's so incredible to see someone who is so confused and spiritually lost, yet who thinks she has direction in life, find out that God has something else for her and discover him. In my mind I was just taking that refresher course to sharpen my nursing skills.

But when I look back on it, I really believe God put me in that class to meet Lori.

That showed me how I need to be open to do what God wants me to do, to give him more freedom to work in my circumstances, to be open to what else he wants to do through me that I am not expecting.

Leading Lori to Christ was incredible for me. It energized my faith. You can do a Bible study lesson in which you get the facts and put them into your mind, but once you live it out it completes the whole picture. You can read what the Bible says about loving others and sharing your faith and the importance of being Christ's ambassador. You can also read about God. But when I can put it into practice, I think, *Wow, now I understand this, or why it says to do this.*

There's nothing more fulfilling than leading someone to Christ. I could have the perfect job in the perfect corporate world, but nothing can compare to or bring as much fulfillment or meaning as seeing someone come to Christ or hearing someone say to me, "Your investment in my life has made such a difference that now I want to do this in the lives of others."

Dwight L. Moody, one of my favorite classic writers, understood how important it is for each of us to reach out to people with the light of Jesus:

Let no one say that he cannot shine because he has not so much influence as some others may have. What God wants you to do is to use the influence you have. . . . Do not let Satan get the advantage of you and make you think that because you cannot do any great thing you cannot do anything at all. . . .

If we only lead one soul to Jesus Christ we may set a stream in motion that will flow on when we are dead and gone. Away up the mountainside there is a little spring. . . . Before long it is a large brook, and then it becomes a broad river. . . . So if you turn one to Christ, that one may turn a hundred; they may turn a thousand, and so the stream, small at first, goes on broadening and deepening as it rolls toward eternity.

May we trust God to use us in whatever ways he wishes, large or small. Because in his eyes, everything we do in obedience is significant, and he will multiply it greatly.

FOR REFLECTION AND DISCUSSION

1. What can we do to become more aware of God's promptings, the opportunities he gives us to love people at work, in our neighborhoods, when we travel on business?

2. In this chapter, Stephen mentions some obstacles that have lessened his sensitivity to the Holy Spirit, including becoming too busy and being self-centered. Which things may be hindering you? What has God taught you about listening to him?

3. Although the story about the conversation with the woman on the airplane has humorous elements, it also illustrates God's perfect timing. Which opportunities to share God's love and truth may be right in front of you right now? How will you respond?

4. How important do you think it is for us to share ourselves—even vulnerable or painful aspects of our lives—with other people? Why?

5. What have you learned about God's leading in the past, through your experiences or those of other people?

6. How can even small conversations or routine situations create opportunities to connect with non-Christians?

7. Reread the quotation by George Müller on pages 79-80. What stands out to you in his statement?

8. If we really believed D. L. Moody's comment (at the end of this chapter) about using the influence we have, in what way(s) might we think differently about our God-given opportunities?

— 5 —

Widening Our Circles of Influence

It is not enough for us to understand our world from afar.

We need to wade into it and rub shoulders with those we desire to reach.

We need to be willing to get our cuffs smudged by the world,

living life with non-Christians on their terms, not ours.

When we enter the world of the men and women around us who don't know Christ,

we lay the groundwork for real communication to take place.

DAVID W. HENDERSON

One fall weekend a friend and I drove from Washington, D.C., to Franklin, West Virginia, to go spelunking. After camping overnight, we entered a small hole in the hillside that a local person had pointed out to us. For amateurs, we were well prepared. We had kneepads, helmets, flashlights, extra batteries and bulbs, water, food, and other essentials. Off we went—kneeling, climbing, crawling our way through various passageways, taking notes so we could find our way out again.

Half an hour later, we stepped into a room about fifty yards long and maybe forty yards wide. As beams from our flashlights bounced off the walls, I stood in awe. I'd never explored a room so big. On a whim, I lit a candle, placed it on a rock in the center of the room and worked my way to a far corner. To my surprise, when we turned off our flashlights that little candle lit up much of that space.

When Jesus described what our relationship to the world is to be like, he used an analogy of light. Knowing that a light must be kindled in the darkness in order to make a difference, he told his disciples why they should let his light shine through them:

> You are the light of the world. A city on a hill cannot be hidden. Neither do people light a lamp and put it under a bowl. Instead they put it on its stand, and it gives light to everyone in the house. In the same way, let your light shine before men, that they may see your good deeds and praise your Father in heaven. (Matthew 5:14-16)

Today as I think about what it means to be a light in my world, memories of that cave come to mind. Each of us is like that little candle. When we befriend non-Christians, we illuminate the truth of Jesus to our spiritually darkening culture. God places each of us where we are for reasons we may never fully understand so that we will shed a little spiritual light on our corners of the world, in our circles of influence.

Jesus spent his earthly life in a relatively small geographical area, yet he profoundly affected the world around him. His light could not be hidden! His life is a powerful example of what it means to be a light to the world. It's possible for each of us to be that kind of light.

Jesus connected with people who were not Christians because he understood them and lived among them. He spoke with them, celebrated with them, helped them with building projects and felt their pain. He walked through alleys and bustling markets. He saw smelly beggars battle for the best locations and depressed lepers standing in the distance. He saw tax collectors' malicious grins and heard religious leaders' pompous prayers. He prayed in desolate mountain regions where shepherds guided their sheep. He mixed with prostitutes, common laborers, high-ranking leaders and slick professors who knew lots about religious doctrine but really didn't know God at all.

I sometimes wonder what Jesus would do if he were invited to a big Christian conference featuring workshops on how to reach non-Christians. Would he attend a seminar on reaching "Boomers," "Busters" or "Gen Xers"? Or would he go outside and talk with the bag lady pushing the cart? Or the businessman having lunch by the fountain? Or the vendor selling magazines and newspapers? Or the woman handing out New Age literature? Or would he help the kitchen staff prepare lunch?

I think it's safe to assume he would gravitate toward people who were in pain or in need of spiritual help. He did this often during his earthly life, as illustrated by his contact with a sobbing widow:

> As he approached the town gate, a dead person was being carried out—the only son of his mother, and she was a widow. . . . When the Lord saw her, his heart went out to her and he said, "Don't cry."
>
> Then he went up and touched the coffin, and those carrying it stood still. He said, "Young man, I say to you, get up!" The dead man sat up and began to talk, and Jesus gave him back to his mother. (Luke 7:12-15)

What is the "world" Jesus mentions in Matthew 5, the world in which we are to reflect his light? The "world" may be the foreign student in your English lit class, the neighbor who grills out a lot on the other side of the fence, the gay activist living in the apartment below you or the physical therapist helping your knee to heal. The "world" is your new friend in the divorce-recovery workshop at church, the man whose car just got a flat tire, the confused student in your statistics class, the woman with the sick baby in the bus station or the lonely employee sitting near you. Perhaps God has given you a burden for singles, long-haul truck drivers, teenage mothers or teenagers in the court system. People all around us need the light of Jesus! They are the world to which we each have been called. And we can choose to widen our spheres of influence by connecting with more non-Christians and expanding our connections with those we already know.

Upon arriving in Athens (see Acts 17:16-34), Paul didn't just walk around, wondering how to connect with Athenians. To widen his circles

COFFEE CONVERSATIONS

Whether or not you are a coffee drinker, coffee shops are great places to meet people and build relationships. Why not stop by the same place several times a week and initiate conversations with other customers?

Roy, an East Coast relative of mine, has met many people at Starbucks. One day he noticed a college student making a model and asked, "Is that a molecular structure model?"

"Very good," she answered. "What are you reading?"

"A book about where to find fulfillment in life," he answered. "The author is a former Hindu who is now a Christian. And I'm a Christian."

"I'm Jewish," she answered.

"By birth or by belief?" he responded.

The two of them ended up talking for quite a while about philosophy, the Old Testament and other subjects. It turned out that she was an avid reader. She invited Roy to attend a philosophy class in which Christianity was discussed. "There are very few Christians in that class," she said. "I had a roommate last year who was a Christian, but she found it hard to talk about her faith with us."

of influence, he jumped right into the thick of things to learn what the Athenians believed and how they felt. He did his research well: he "reasoned in the synagogue with the Jews and the God-fearing Greeks, as well as in the marketplace day by day with those who happened to be there." He met brilliant thinkers of his day and common people, and he proclaimed the gospel publicly.

Soon this preacher of God's Word began to attract quite a bit of attention. Philosophers argued with him, then invited him to share his "strange ideas." Having prepared for this invitation by walking with God, studying Scripture and observing the world around him, Paul began an impromptu speech by noting that the Athenians were religious. How did he know that? Not only had he listened to them and looked at their idols, he had noticed one particular altar that bore this inscription: "TO AN UN-KNOWN GOD." He used that inscription to introduce the gospel.

How did Paul do this? By using common images and phrases the Athenians understood, he built a bridge of communication that allowed him to speak about God as the Creator, the need for humankind to repent, the coming judgment and Jesus' resurrection. Paul had prepared himself by doing his biblical and cultural homework.

In *How Now Shall We Live?* Chuck Colson writes about the importance of connecting with people in ways they understand:

> When advancing the biblical perspective in public debate, we ought to interpret biblical truth in ways that appeal to the common good. So although we believe that Scripture is God's inerrant revelation, we do not have to derive all arguments directly from Scripture. . . . We must be able to speak to the scientist in the language of science, to the artist in the language of art, to the politician in the language of politics.

EACH OF US HAS AN IMPORTANT ROLE

As I watch NASCAR drivers jockeying for position while traveling more than one hundred miles per hour faster than my Honda will ever go, I can't help but think of all the different components working together to keep each car operating. Each part—an airfoil, spark plug, lug nut, brake cable—is important. Every component must do its part in order for the car to respond well during a race.

The apostle Paul described the body of Christ in a way that emphasized its unity and diversity:

> The body is a unit, though it is made up of many parts; and though all its parts are many, they form one body. . . . If the whole body were an ear, where would the sense of smell be? But in fact God

has arranged the parts in the body, every one of them, just as he wanted them to be. If they were all one part, where would the body be? As it is, there are many parts, but one body. . . . Now you are the body of Christ, and each one of you is a part of it. (1 Corinthians 12:12, 17-20, 27)

Through the years, I've met many Christians in the United States and overseas. The eyes of some dance with joy as they describe what God is teaching them and his faithfulness. They open up their Bible easily to share meaningful verses. They describe how God has met them during painful times when they didn't know if they could keep going, including times of doubt when they didn't know where to turn. They share hard-earned lessons of obedience and humility, battles with lust and pride, marital struggles that brought them to their knees, and deep questions. Through it all, the good and the bad and the ugly, they are growing spiritually. They don't have all the answers, but they look to God as their primary source of love, joy, peace and the other fruit of the Spirit. They love him and trust in his character.

Other Christians are quite different. They seem to avoid talking about God. When asked what they have been learning about him, they joylessly recite a sentence or two. When struggles come, they seem to cope just like anybody else, without much thought of God. They seem to have little fruit of the Spirit in their life, and this lack of fruit is costly.

In order to grow spiritually and be an effective witness to people, I've learned that I need the support of other Christians who strive to know and obey God, who look to him for strength and hope and joy. I need their encouragement. I need their help when I encounter particularly difficult situations or when someone I'm connecting with needs something I'm unable to provide. (For example, the wife of a non-Christian friend needs counseling help from another woman for a period of time.) I need the body of Christ—each and every part.

If you haven't found a church to attend, keep looking. No matter how strong you may think you are, you need the love and insightful perspective of godly Christians. You need to see God's love and joy overflowing from others' lives when you are feeling dry spiritually and are discouraged. You also need at least one godly person to whom you can be accountable, someone who loves you just the way you are, will pray regularly for you and will encourage you to keep growing spiritually so what you have to share with non-Christians remains vibrant, genuine and exciting.

It isn't easy to take time out to be alone with God. I often find it hard, honestly, to find time to pray and read the Bible. I get caught up in writing paragraphs like these, meeting with people, doing errands, answering correspondence, trying to conserve enough time for my family and many other things you probably do too. Worse yet, sometimes I find myself minimizing my need for spiritual food. I sometimes think I can keep myself running in my own strength.

ORGANIZE A BLOCK PARTY

Everybody has to eat, and few people will turn down the chance to grill burgers and sample other people's tasty dishes. In one neighborhood, a random gathering of people on the Fourth of July became a tradition. The residents closed off the street for a block party and brought their favorite foods. From about noon until dark, neighbors talked, threw Frisbees and played with each other's children.

If you live in an apartment, see if you can reserve the clubhouse or block off part of the parking lot. Or arrange for everyone to meet at a nearby park.

But time and again, I discover I can't. And I'm thankful for Christians who in word and deed encourage me to keep focusing on the essentials.

When my spiritual well is deep and I drink from it often, the water I drink and can share with other people is clean, cool and refreshing. Then, praise God, I am—in his strength—a man of influence.

When my spiritual well is shallow, the water I drink and share is tepid, dirty and far from satisfying. My light grows dim; my salt loses its flavor.

As I age, I find myself asking different kinds of questions: Which people might I be able to share God's love with if I pray for them regularly and keep my eyes open for opportunities to reach out to them? Which sins will I avoid if I read the Bible every day and "put on the armor of God" (Ephesians 6)? How much more sensitive will I be if I allow God to keep filling me with himself daily, so I don't need to take so much from other people or find temporary substitutes for my lack of love, joy, peace, patience and self-control? How much more courage will I have to stand up for Jesus when it's not a popular thing to do? How much more of God's joy will I have, no matter how tough things become?

> *Getting personal with God begins with knowing.*
> *The more deeply we know the more fully we can love, and the more fully we love the more completely we can serve.*
>
> PETER DEISON

In order to share God's living water effectively with non-Christians, I need to know him better. I need the spiritual well that becomes deeper and more satisfying the more I draw from it.

FINDING JOY IN OUR UNIQUENESS

As a part of the body of Christ, each of us is unique, and this uniqueness is expressed in everything we do. Some of us are gifted in athletics, so it might make sense for us to play in tournaments with non-Christians or make new friends while snowboarding. Some of us are couch potatoes who would enjoy inviting non-Christians to watch and discuss movies. Some of us enjoy reading and discussing bestselling books. Some of us enjoy walking with friends in a park. The list could go on and on. What's important to note here is that *we* are the church—a vital way God chooses to reveal his character and truth. The diversity of our gifts is not evident just when we go into church buildings; it carries over into everything we do and say, including being God's witnesses wherever we are. God has built us like that.

Every Christian plays an important role in going "into all the world" and proclaiming the "good news" (Mark 16:15). We each have unique circles of relationships and interests, abilities and resources, dreams and experiences. God wants us to use our influence *intentionally* within these circles to penetrate our culture for his kingdom.

Perhaps you are active in your neighborhood, meeting newcomers or setting up young-mother activities. Maybe you work in an office every day, demonstrating Jesus through word and deed. Whether you realize it or not, you are being a witness for Jesus wherever you are, in whatever you do. And you'll impact people I'll never meet, in places far from my small office in Colorado.

No matter where we live, what type of friends we have, how much money we make, how old or healthy we are, what our ethnic backgrounds are, what kinds of dreams we have, how long we've been Christians, we can intentionally and appropriately demonstrate and share what God is doing in our lives. We have experienced his love, forgiveness, guidance, hope and truth, and these are worth sharing! Maybe we just mention God or the Bible in passing, giving people the opportunity to ask curious questions and open the door to learning more. Maybe we have the opportunity to share more of what God has done and is doing in our lives. Maybe we mention a biblical principle that has made a big difference in our business.

It's easy to forget that who we are in Christ, day after day, influences countless people. Our attitudes, character, generosity and willingness to listen make a great difference, even when we aren't aware of it. And when we are willing to be vulnerable about our weaknesses in relation to our faith, people notice that too.

While researching this book, I met Carol Mayberry, a teacher who has built grassroots, enduring relationships with non-Christians for many years. She talked with me about how important it is to be real, to be willing to tell others about challenges with which we struggle. As she pointed out, people really do want to know how our faith in God makes a difference in practical aspects of life. "People don't necessarily want to know how you met God or why you think you are connected to God," she mused. "They want to know how come you seem really happy every day. How come you don't seem super-anxious over a bad situation—or maybe you are and you share about it in a vulnerable way. Sharing my story, and listening to someone else's story, reminds us that we are all human, that we share our humanity together. Yes, I'm human, I struggle, and this is how I deal with it, with God's help."

When you and I take the opportunity to love non-Christians within our circles of influence, we will discover that we have more in common with them than we first thought. Our lives will resonate with their's. Our stereotypes of them will evaporate. We will learn from them; they will learn from us. The lives of Christians and non-Christians often interconnect, and God desires to use that interconnection in powerful ways.

Jesus knew the impact that ordinary people like you and me have. That's why he commissioned twelve of them to evangelize the world. And they did! Just as they were commissioned to make an eternal difference in people's lives, we are commissioned too.

God is always searching for someone just like you who will be his ambassador, his representative. Not just in a Sunday school class, as a preacher or as a missionary. Yes, he calls people to these strategic places, but he wants us to realize that all of life is spiritual and to take his love and truth everywhere. Wherever you are, you have a unique opportunity to represent God—in a high-rise building, in a small neighborhood, in your home, on a college campus, anywhere in the world. People all around you haven't met Jesus personally, and you have the opportunity to reflect Jesus to each of them, intentionally. What a privilege.

When you leave a grocery store, do you greet the cashier with an eye-catching smile? Do you drop a note to the auto mechanic who treated you well or the teacher who made a huge difference in your child's life? Often it's the small things done in love that really reflect Jesus. They are not hard to do; they just require a little time and the loving awareness that comes when we allow God's character to overflow from our lives.

You are very important to God. How you respond to people around you matters a great deal. Don't forget that, even during the heat of difficulties.

DISCOVERING OUR CIRCLES OF INFLUENCE

You may be a single mother with two children, a maintenance worker, a company president, a retail clerk, a retired person who loves teens, a politician, a businessperson or an outfitter in northern Wyoming. Whoever you are, wherever you live, whatever you do, strive to be a servant of Jesus who brings glory to God. By the Holy Spirit's power working in and through you, God can use you to make an eternal difference in people's lives. Choose to become involved. Choose to walk closely with God. Read the Bible and pray regularly so what you have to share is fresh, alive and relevant. Choose to think about what Jesus would do in situations you face.

To start sharing Jesus' love, we don't have to travel far from home, attend evangelism seminars, read certain books or be great speakers. We can start relating to people we know right now, with what we know, in natural and loving ways. I work at home, not with coworkers, yet within the past week I have had the following contacts with people, some of whom are not Christians:

- went to a movie with an acquaintance
- spoke briefly to a neighbor walking on the county road near our home
- gave mail to a neighbor who had been gone for a few days
- listened to a man describe what he thinks a "Christian" is
- talked with the owner of a tire store
- attended a workshop on wildfire mitigation and visited with a Mormon friend who helped to set up the meeting
- spoke with a woman at the front desk of an exercise club who is getting married soon
- discussed a book contrasting Christianity and Buddhism with a physical therapist
- set up a lunch meeting with a non-Christian who attended my surprise birthday party

- discussed woodcutting options with the father of one of my daughter's friends

These people are like me in many ways, and for some reason they and many others have been brought into my life. Now I must choose how to respond. Some, like the woman who got married and no longer works at the exercise club, I may not see again. But others I will. And with God's help, I can be sensitive in discovering ways to connect with them.

Whom do you talk with regularly? See in the corner café? Visit with on the telephone? Pass in the hallway at work or school? Push weights next to in the health club? Talk with in the parking lot of your child's school? Chances are, you are in contact with far more people than I am! Like a rock thrown into the waters of a pond, your contacts with people ripple out to the world.

Think about who God has created you to be and where he has placed you. Which opportunities might you have to share Jesus' love and truth this week? Perhaps you are a skilled musician, able to reflect Christ to a diverse teen audience; an accountant who can help people learn and ap-

BECOME ACTIVE IN A COMMUNITY GROUP OR CAUSE

Almost every neighborhood has groups active in community affairs. Perhaps you could help start a crime-prevention group. Or maybe an issue is coming up at a public hearing. The keys here are participation and common interests.

Once our school district wanted to make a boundary change and force children to switch schools. Even though the decision wouldn't affect us, we chose to become involved. We spoke out on behalf of others in our community and telephoned the news media so that the issue would receive citywide attention. Our participation had a strong impact on at least one family, who realized we had responded out of loving concern for them and not because we had anything to gain for ourselves.

ply biblical financial principles; a computer genius who can help writers like me keep their e-mail systems working; an actor or actress, able to earn the right to speak to others in theater; an administrative assistant who can bring God's joy into coworkers' lives when the business is going well and when it's struggling.

Perhaps you can touch the life of a man or woman you know who is addicted to alcohol, sex or work; visit someone in jail; discuss important subjects with other students in your dormitory; regularly spend time with skiers, hunters, fishermen or backpackers; connect well with young mothers in your neighborhood; till people's gardens in the spring or shovel their driveways in the winter; or develop relationships with people who attend your child's sporting events week after week.

Use who God has created you to be—your strengths and your weaknesses—and the gifts and resources he has given you to make a difference in your unique circles of influence. Ask God to guide you to non-Christians and to help you recognize ways in which you can reflect the light of Jesus. If you do, you will reach far more people during your lifetime than you could ever imagine.

STAN'S STORY

Stan discovered the influence he could have almost as soon as he became a Christian. He grew up in a Jewish family. During his teenage years, he became pretty wild and hung out with friends of many backgrounds—Catholic, Baptist, secular, you name it. But as he puts it, "I never really saw the life of Christ in them. Kids would tell their parents they were going to Mass, then go down to the beach with me to party. Even the son of a prominent pastor in town joined in. I didn't see any reason to be a Christian because I didn't see anything attractive to me."

Desiring a change, Stan joined the U.S. Air Force and kept partying. But God was working through Christians who widened their circles of influence to include him. "At a duty station in Oklahoma," he says, "I started meeting people called Christians at the base barber shop and the exchange. I even ended up working with a Christian every day. They'd share their lives and faith with me, trying to talk about Israel and salvation. And I started to see a common thread: they had a love for each other I'd never seen before. The love I'd always seen was so superficial. These guys were committed to each other and loved each other, and that really drew me into the body of Christ.

"One night I accepted Jesus as my Savior. That decision brought me into a family, into a community, and I'd never felt like I'd belonged in a community before."

Several weeks later, Stan's Christian friends invited him to become involved in a Saturday-night outreach ministry. They recognized the influence he could, in turn, have on others.

The world is not impressed by our eloquent argumentation, nor is it convinced by our elaborate explanations. The world wants to see reality in a person's life. It only takes notice of that which it cannot produce—a life transformed by righteousness. But only God can produce that—which is why Christianity is the most revolutionary force in the world. It promises to effect true life-change.

HOWARD HENDRICKS

At first, being brand new to the faith, I didn't do much. But soon I was learning Christian songs and playing my guitar. And I started speaking about how Jesus had changed my life.

Word spread about the outreach, and every Saturday night more Air Force folks started showing up. That's where I met Sue.

I'll never forget her. She was in her early twenties. Having grown up in a broken home and been abused, she was hungry for love and very promiscuous. She hardly opened her mouth when she talked and kept her head down. She was so withdrawn that she wasn't attractive.

She came to a Saturday meeting about five weeks after I became a Christian. As I shared with the group what Jesus had done for me, she listened quietly and later raised her hand to show that she had received Jesus. Immediately her countenance changed dramatically. Joy filled her face. She had a peace she'd never felt before and felt free because God had forgiven her sins. It was a time of rejoicing for everyone.

All I did was share my story! I was amazed that God used me like that, and I felt really good inside.

Sue attended the outreach regularly after that and grew spiritually. She began to recount her testimony (nobody coached her), openly confessing details of her past. Almost immediately other people came to Christ too, after hearing her tell what God had done. The circles of influence just kept widening—and no doubt they still are!

ANOTHER REASON TO WIDEN OUR CIRCLES OF INFLUENCE

Years ago I came to understand that God wanted me to share the gospel message with people. I knew about the Great Commission—Jesus' command to go into the world—and I hoped that I could in a small way reflect Jesus' love so people would be attracted to him. But I now understand that God also commanded me to go into my world because he knew what would happen to *me* when I shared his truth with people.

No matter how many books I read, how many church services I attend and how many Christians I interact with regularly, there are lessons I can learn only when I reach out to non-Christians. It is then that I am forced to articulate my views in ways that people who are quite different from me can understand. That I am challenged to love people who aren't easy to befriend and love. That I must read and reread Scripture to find answers to difficult questions. That I am required to listen intently. That I am more motivated to pray, because I realize how little I can accomplish on my own. That I become more aware of the weaknesses in me that only God can strengthen. That I am reminded of my need to walk in faith outside the boat, as Peter did. That I am aware that everything I say and do is observed and may make an eternal difference in someone's life. That I realize how little I know and become free to learn from others, including people whose lives are radically different from mine.

In short, when I share God's love and truth with people around me, I grow closer to him and my faith deepens. I am greatly stretched, often in uncomfortable ways that prove to be beneficial in the end.

"I think we need evangelism," says Randy Raysbrook of The Navigators, "just as much as the lost do. When I do evangelism training, I say, 'You need to share the gospel for *your* sake. You need to share it in order to obey God for the sake of others. Connecting with spiritually lost people deepens our faith, increases our spiritual sensitivity, and makes us reevaluate our belief system and learn about other people who are different from us. We come out better!'"

Today we each must make a basic choice. Are we willing to intentionally connect with non-Christians? Often we share the same environments with them. When we notice that we've been spending most of our time around Christians, will we choose to go where non-   Christians are? Maybe that will take us to a blues or bluegrass concert on a Saturday night or to the beach on Sunday. Usually they are not coming to our churches, so we need to take Jesus to them. To befriend them on their own turf. To try to see things from their perspectives. Are we willing to focus on Jesus and allow him to use us wherever we live? Of course I'm not saying we should follow them into topless clubs, séances or other places where God doesn't want us to go. But whenever it is appropriate, we need to spend more time in their worlds and less time inviting them to enter ours.

Bill Hybels, senior pastor at Willow Creek Community Church, realized that he and his fellow pastors needed to make intentional commitments to connect with non-Christians on their turf:

If we're serious about reaching the non-Christian, most of us are going to have to take some giant steps. I have suggested for many years that our pastors at Willow Creek find authentic interest areas in their lives—tennis, golf, jogging, sailing, mechanical work, whatever—and pursue these in a totally secular realm. Instead of joining a church league softball team, why not join a park district team? Instead of working out in the church gym, shoot baskets at the YMCA. On vacation, don't go to a Bible conference but to some state park where the guy in the next campsite is going to bring over his six-pack and sit at your picnic table.

HOW DO WE BUILD FRIENDSHIPS WITH NON-CHRISTIANS?

Take the first steps:

- Be friendly.
- Learn and use the person's name.
- Show sincere interest in what the person says and does.
- Listen attentively.

Build relationship:

- Make a conscious effort to stay in touch, in person or by phone. Show your availability without pressuring.
- Invite the person to join you in an activity you enjoy—perhaps a walk, movie, shopping.
- Invite the person to stop over for dinner or dessert, if appropriate. (Such one-on-one activities work best with someone of your same sex.)
- Express sincere interest in his or her interests and ideas, and be affirming whenever you can.
- Share aspects of your life naturally, without an agenda. It's important for him or her to feel you are being open and honest about what's really going on in your life.

Keep adding relational links:

- Show that you value the friendship.
- Be willing to help in practical ways.
- Go out of your way to do something thoughtful for him or her.
- Receive any kindness shown you with appreciation.
- Build on your love for, and appreciation of, the person. Build on what you've talked about previously.

- Ask his or her advice, if appropriate.
- Keep listening, and ask sincere questions that show you care.

GETTING STARTED

I don't know any formulas that are guaranteed to help everybody start making a difference within their circles of influence. If such formulas did exist, they'd probably be quite long and inflexible. But I have found two principles to be quite helpful, even though they may at first seem obvious.

Build on common interests. Relationships with non-Christians, like other relationships, typically revolve around common interests and felt needs. And it takes work—and sometimes opening yourself up to a new interest or being more sensitive to needs—to discover and cultivate interests you can share with non-Christians.

This morning I spoke with Craig, a computer whiz who does consulting and runs a small business. To me, computers are a necessary evil. I woefully underutilize all the gigs, rams, bytes and beeps hiding inside them. But I'm stretching to understand Craig and his world—and in the process my world is being enhanced.

Soon after I first met him, Craig asked for help in solving a tough business issue. We worked it out together, and in a sense I earned the right to speak with him about deeper issues. Since then we have spent quite a few hours together.

Sometimes you and I will connect with people in ways we'd never expect. Carol Mayberry told me this story:

> During a class I was taking in graduate school, an African American woman kept turning around and staring at me when certain topics came up.
>
> Finally I asked her, "What are you doing? You keep looking at me."
>
> "I want to know what you think about when certain subjects come up," she said. "I know you are a Christian, and I'm just watching your face."

Today, years later, they remain friends and still discuss important issues.

Growing up not far from Chicago, I was exposed to blues music and learned to love it. Today I play blues as well as country and bluegrass on my harmonicas from time to time, and that has opened up opportunities to meet and build relationships with other musicians. While playing with several local musicians, I carpooled with a guy who used to tour professionally, and we discussed such topics as drugs, marriage and family priorities. Although these days he is quite busy in a new real-estate career, we occasionally talk on the phone, and at his invitation I played with him and his band one evening. He and his wife have come over for dinner, and it's about time to give him another call to stay in touch.

CONNECT ON THEIR TURF

Many non-Christians I know don't want much, if anything, to do with the organized church. They don't want to attend Sunday services or special evangelistic meetings. But they'll discuss significant topics over dessert in our home, ponder the beauty of creation while fishing for trout and join us in doing other fun activities. And I don't think the non-Christians we know are unique.

Some churches, like the Brooklyn Tabernacle in New York City, regularly attract non-Christians, who are drawn to the testimonies of changed lives, the Bible teaching that connects with who they are, and the praise, worship and prayer. But from my vantage point, some of us still place far too much evangelistic emphasis on trying to get non-Christians to enter our churches rather than creatively figuring out how to go to them. I've read articles and books for pastors on how to attract various segments of culture—children, singles, men who are athletic, at-home moms, teenagers who raise pigs in 4-H (just kidding)—to church. Although the resulting programs no doubt make a positive difference, I wish more Christians would focus on how they can penetrate the worlds of non-Christians in genuine, sincere ways. I know God keeps challenging me to think along these lines.

We have great opportunities to go where non-Christians are. There are as many outreach opportunities as we can imagine. The gray suggestion boxes scattered throughout this book represent only a fraction of the possible ways we can connect. If non-Christians are not coming to us, we must go to them!

This might mean walking over to someone working on a car, taking walks with a woman who just moved into your neighborhood, inviting several non-Christians to go backpacking or skiing with you, starting a book discussion group, helping someone fix a lamp, or going to see a movie and discussing it afterward. Think of the possibilities. It could even mean going with someone to a NASCAR race on Sunday.

Although some older methods of reaching non-Christians don't work nearly as well as they once did, many things remain the same. Non-Christians long for personal relationships, just as we do. They also search for answers to problems and wonder about spiritual issues.

HOLD A NEIGHBORHOOD GARAGE SALE

Most people have items they'd like to sell or give away. Invite your neighbors, friends and acquaintances to participate. It's a great way to meet new people. You may even want to furnish the driveway. If you live in an apartment complex, see if you can use a corner of the parking lot. Arrange for at least one adult from each participating family to spend time at the sale, and don't be surprised if you end up talking with neighbors you hardly knew as if you were longtime buddies.

Peter Mayberry, Carol's husband, who has led "friendship evangelism" seminars in churches, observes:

Many Christians don't think they can relate to non-Christians, and they miss the basic issues people are longing for—connection with other people. That's what my wife and I are finding in our neighborhood Bible study. These folks just want to be connected.

They are looking for people to relate to and wanting to be part of a community where the emphasis is on establishing beneficial relationships with one another, where there is some intentionality to love people well. We have found that people in our home Bible study are very responsive. They do want to connect, to be around Christians who care for them and to care in return.

God has equipped us to do the work he calls us to do. Now we have to decide how we'll respond.

FOR REFLECTION AND DISCUSSION

1. Which of your interests, hobbies or activities bring you in touch with non-Christians? How might what you read in this chapter influence your communication with them?

2. Which person(s) might God want you to begin connecting with in a more significant way this coming week?

3. What have you already learned about connecting with people in your circles of influence? How can you put your experience to better use in the days and weeks ahead?

4. How can a Christian develop genuine love for non-Christians?

5. What are some creative ways in which you can build sincere relationships with non-Christians?

6. Which activities in which you regularly participate provide opportunities to invite people to go with you?

7. How much are you using your home as an opportunity to connect with non-Christians? (Invitations to share a meal? A game night? An evangelistic Bible study?)

Leading the Way
Through the Cultural Maze

As soon as truth ceases to be a binding authority that stands above a man,

it becomes a merely servile function whose purpose is to

give some kind of legitimacy to his interests.

HELMUT THIELICKE

Rachel, a college student, enrolled in a class in which small groups of students discussed what they valued in life, things beyond themselves. A strong Christian, Rachel told the group, "I value my faith in God."

A classmate, Carol, agreed: "Yeah, I also value my faith. It's in the spirit of the universe."

"No," Rachel said, "I'm talking about something completely different. My faith is in God; I pray, and my prayers are answered."

"I pray to the crystals by my bed," Carol said, "and I get answers too—for jobs, health or whatever."

"No, my faith in God is totally different," Rachel answered. "It gives me real inner peace, a sense of belonging."

"Right!" exclaimed Carol. "So does mine."

Rachel later approached a college ministry leader for help in sorting out the conversation. She didn't understand how two entirely different views of God and the world could appear to be so similar. Her confusion is understandable.

Today many people like Carol pursue their own brands of spirituality built on *subjective* truth. They commonly say things like these:

- "Everybody's faith is the same in the end."
- "Religions are different but similar."
- "Nothing is eternal, infinite or right for everybody. We each have to choose which truth to believe, to figure out our own paths and what feels right."
- "If it works for you, great! If not, find something that does."
- "The divine is in all of us."

Among non-Christians for whom tolerance is a primary value, there's strong resistance to any faith or religion that says it's the only way to God and thereby excludes the beliefs of others. Os Guinness addresses this powerfully:

> To hold that there is one God, and no god but God, is to feel the force of the theological discrimination of God and His truth over against all other truth claims and moral judgments. . . . Clearly our modern culture is no friend to this point. Tolerance has so recoiled from intolerance as to become intolerant itself. Meanwhile, relativism has become the last absolute, . . . and glorying in being open-minded has become closed-minded. Because nothing is true or false, everything is considered equal—except a truth that does not claim that everything else is true.

Furthermore, many non-Christians have joyous, compelling stories to tell of how a supreme being, dynamic force or "other" influenced their lives spiritually. They describe peace they have received, answered prayers and problems their spirituality has helped them overcome. And some of them—even agnostics who have "suspended" their faith—are quite evangelistic in sharing their spiritual views with other people.

Satan, the father of lies, is the master counterfeiter! He is especially active today. Millions of people are trying with growing intensity to discover religious truth that works in their lives. So we must be prepared to face truth-related issues with sensitivity as we build relationships with non-Christians and share *the* Truth with them. We must not forget that Jesus said, "I am *the* way and *the* truth and *the* life" (John 14:6). He didn't say "*a* way, *a* truth and *a* life." That set him—and therefore us today— apart from mainstream culture's beliefs.

Because we have God's truth, in Jesus and the Bible, we are free to pay careful attention to the beliefs of other people and to respond to those people in sensitive, loving ways. Sadly, though, our reactions often seem to be quite different.

When I was an agnostic, struggling with truth-related issues, some Christians almost seemed to enjoy hammering me with the Bible. "How can you believe what you believe?" they'd ask. "The Bible says . . ." When I tried to talk with them in depth, they'd act as if they had all the answers rather than as if they were on a journey of spiritual discovery and were exploring issues with me. They did believe that Jesus is the Truth, but they communicated their convictions offensively. I didn't want to hear answers; I already knew the party lines. I wanted to hear and evaluate people's perspectives and to make my decisions about what to believe without pressure and condemnation. I also wanted people to love me for who I was and respect where I was in my spiritual journey. Ironically, I usually found more acceptance among other "seekers" than among Christians, who often substituted criticism and emotion for critical thinking and love.

I still cringe sometimes when I hear some so-called Christian messages on radio and television. No wonder many of our non-Christian friends are defensive about what they believe when Christians are around.

A few years ago, my wife and I saw firsthand the importance of earning the right, through caring relationships with non-Christians, to share the truth of Jesus. We also were reminded of why non-Christians must always be approached in love, no matter how heated a discussion may become.

We signed up to participate in what were called Dialogue Dinners. Animosity had been building in the Colorado Springs area; gays, lesbians, atheists and people committed to secularism felt uneasy about the growing population of conservative Christians, who appeared to be judging everyone else by the Bible's "intolerant" standards. In response, a local organization, built on "celebrating diversity" and supported and run by people openly opposed to the Bible's claim to objective truth, launched these dinners in order to give non-Christians and Christians opportunities to meet one another and discuss important topics in participants' homes.

My wife and I grew to love the participants in our group, which included an atheist and several agnostics. We met for several years. One evening a National Public Radio host interviewed our group, and the interview was aired during a week-long series on cultural values. At one point during that taped discussion, I said something like this: "We meet together in each other's homes and enjoy good discussions and meals. We have become friends. But fundamentally we have very different beliefs about the nature of truth." On the surface, participants agreed on many things. But on a deeper level, the non-Christians' views of truth diverged radically from biblical truth.

Later, after the group cordially disbanded more than a year later than originally scheduled, I realized how much it had affected all of us. The Christians had come to recognize how, and sometimes why, the non-Christians believed what they believed. The non-Christians had been drawn a bit closer to Jesus and his love and had come to recognize that Christians can be thoughtful and compassionate. And I had begun to really understand and love non-Christians who were dedicated to challenging the Christian worldview.

Sadly, truth-related discussions about spirituality often cause rifts between people. A good friend of mine, who doesn't know Jesus, once sidestepped a discussion about spiritual truth by saying, "Religion exaggerates differences," and then changing the subject. He didn't want our opposing views of truth to damage our relationship. However, I remain committed to demonstrating Jesus' love to him in ways he *can* receive and respect. One of these days we may have that discussion about spiritual truth, particularly if I ask him questions about his background and beliefs rather than being too eager to emphasize mine.

Discussions about spiritual truth can exaggerate differences, but that doesn't mean we shouldn't attempt to communicate biblical truth. Quite the contrary! There is so much we can learn from non-Christians and so much they can learn from us.

I have seen great communication take place between non-Christians and Christians. However, I have witnessed much more harmful wounding than loving dialogue.

We Christians often come across as being dogmatic and even arrogant, projecting this message: "I've got the truth, and you need to accept it and be set free." Often we act as if we have all the spiritual truth and no longer need to search for spiritual truth, and anyone who disagrees with us is wrong. Although Jesus clearly states that he is the only legitimate way to God, do we really want to communicate that our spiritual journey is over as soon as we become Christians? Non-Christians understandably are more drawn toward people who listen, learn and love than toward people who appear to have all the answers and don't appreciate the viewpoints of others. Do we really want to push them away? What does it mean to love people who have opposing perspectives from ours?

If we Christians are to effectively communicate with non-Christians, first and foremost we need to build sincere relationships with them, or at least earn their respect, and seek to understand what they believe about truth. We need to listen to what they say about the truths they believe and express genuine interest in them as people. And sometimes it is better to love and listen than to compare and contrast their beliefs to what the Bible says.

We also need to try to understand *why* they believe the truths they believe. Often, as I've discovered in myself, people's real reasons for believing as they do relate to painful events that drew or even dropkicked them away from Christians and the Christian faith.

For quite a while after I became a Christian, I debated with non-Christians to discover their beliefs rather than simply asking them what and why they believe and showing love through building relationships. Sometimes all I accomplished was further reinforcing their stereotypes of what Christians are like. I didn't see the harm I was causing.

> *We believe in truth. For that reason, we ought to honor our honest differences with others (and among ourselves) by recognizing them and seeking understanding. The assumption that truth exists, after all, frees us from fearing differences and from ignoring the differences that exist.*
>
> S. D. GAEDE

The apostle Paul, who had a mile-long pedigree of educational successes including years of study under an influential rabbi, realized that words alone are not enough to convince people of the gospel's truth. "My message and my preaching," he wrote in 1 Corinthians 2:4-5, "were not with wise and persuasive words, but with a demonstration of the Spirit's power, so that your faith might not rest on men's wisdom, but on God's power."

In *The Case for Christ* and *The Case for Faith*, Lee Strobel offers effective evidences in support of the Christian faith and encourages readers to investigate them. But no matter how good those evidences are, does Lee actually "save" people? No. That's God's work. We must give non-Christians the freedom to struggle with spiritual issues and even say *no* to Jesus. At the same time, we can continue to pray for them, love them in practical ways, openly share what God is doing in our lives and let God do the rest in his timing.

BLURRING LINES OF TRUTH

If we are to communicate successfully with non-Christians, we must understand how and why issues of truth concerning God and spirituality are becoming more blurred and indistinct, like a washed-out watercolor print.

The gulf continues to widen between Christians and non-Christians

Table 1. Different Attitudes Toward Truth

Moral Absolutism

Orthodox	Without moral absolutes there are no guidelines for right and wrong. Certain moral absolutes exist, and we can know them.
Progressive	Moral absolutes are too general to be consistently ethical or compassionate in different situations. Each individual has an individual sense of morality.

Abortion

Orthodox	Abortion is murder and should not be legal. The life of the pre-born child is of paramount importance.
Progressive	It is not clear when human life begins, and each woman should have the right to control her reproductive choices. Women's access to legal abortions is of paramount importance.

Christian America

Orthodox	America was founded as a Christian nation and should remain true to Christian principles. America has a Judeo-Christian heritage, which it should honor rather than deny.
Progressive	America was founded as a pluralistic nation and combined values should inform policy. The riches of democracy are rooted more in Greek and Roman thought than in Christianity or any other religion.

Morality

Orthodox	Christianity presents a codified moral code for this country; without this code "anything goes." Morality is rooted in the Ten Commandments.
Progressive	In a pluralistic nation we must recognize that there are different bases for morality and strive to understand values held in common and values that differ. Every culture has its own basis of morality, and they are equally valid.

This material was originally included in a handout provided to Food for Thought Dialogue Dinner participants in Colorado Springs, Colorado, in the mid-1990s. Used by permission.

concerning the nature of truth. A handout provided to help foster discussion among participants in the Dialogue Dinners included a chart summarizing these differences (see table 1). The "orthodox" statements intend to summarize Christians' perspectives; the "progressive" statements aim to summarize others' views. Consider the differences.

Although the handout was not designed to be all-encompassing, such differences concerning the nature of truth are showing up everywhere in our culture. Our society is moving further and further away from viewing the Bible as fully inspired, objective truth from God that applies to everyone and all of reality. Many people believe that anyone who claims to have such truth from God is ignorant, a fool or an intolerant bigot.

RELATE CHRIST TO CONTEMPORARY EVENTS

After the events of September 11, 2001, many Americans became interested in learning about Islam. A pastor in Illinois who had grown up Muslim gave a talk on Islam at his church, and many people from the local community attended. His presentation allowed them not only to learn about Islam but also to learn about aspects of Christianity and to ask questions.

And a growing number of Christians have also bought into the concept that there is no such thing as capital-T Truth, only variations of small-t truth. They have come to accept their faith as only one of many equally valid faiths.

Whenever we refer to the Bible, however, we encourage people to pay attention to it. We can't make them believe it is God's Word or apply its truths in daily life, but we can encourage them to read it, evaluate its claims and promises and historicity, and perhaps become more open to discovering the personal Jesus who longs to be in relationship with them.

It's fascinating to talk with different types of people and find out what they believe. I meet people who believe that people are inherently good, yet always lock their doors. I meet people who think the Bible is irrelevant, but haven't read much or any of it. I meet people who promote people's freedom to create their own lifestyles, yet get angry when someone in a nearby apartment plays the stereo too loudly or works as a logger for a lumber company. I meet people who don't believe in the fall of Adam and sin, but feel guilty sometimes—and won't live in a high-crime neighborhood. I meet people who have many traditional, biblically based values such as the importance of honesty and helping poor people, but reject the idea that such values are rooted in the Bible. I meet people who want to be free of religious restrictions and want the freedom to make their own choices, but don't like it when they have to bear the negative consequences of another person's choice.

These inconsistencies don't surprise me nearly as much, however, as the number of people who, having recognized inconsistencies (or even falsehoods) in their beliefs, smile or shrug their shoulders, believing that such contradictions are okay. No one can know everything anyway, they reason, and life is full of contradictions and unanswerables.

It's one thing to criticize non-Christians' thinking from a distance; it's another to love them enough to study cultural trends and try to understand what it's like to walk in their shoes. Imagine, for a moment, that you believe that the Bible is not God's Word, that God can't communicate personally to human beings, and that there is no such thing as sin, heaven or hell. Let's say you also believe Jesus lived on earth and was a great teacher but was not the Son of God. On what might you base your view of truth? Would you pursue absolute moral relativism—the ultimate belief that no moral standards universally apply to all of human reality? Would you turn to pluralism? How would you respond if Christians tried to argue you into the kingdom of God?

PLURALISM: INFLUENCING CHRISTIANS AND NON-CHRISTIANS ALIKE

Pluralism is a word we need to understand as we build relationships with non-Christians and seek to deepen our own Christian faith. Pluralism is influencing many people's perspectives on truth, whether they realize it or not. Here's how the concept is summarized by David Brooks, a contributing editor at *Newsweek* and senior editor of the *Weekly Standard*:

> The spiritual pluralist believes that the universe cannot be reduced to one natural order, one divine plan. Therefore, there cannot be one path to salvation. There are varieties of happiness, distinct moralities, and different ways to virtue. What's more, no one ever really arrives at a complete answer to the deepest questions or to faith. It is a voyage. We are forever incomplete, making choices, exploring, creating. . . . The proper spiritual posture, therefore, is to be open-minded about new choices and paths, to be empathetic toward new opinions, temperaments and worldviews. . . . All that is required is that people of good faith seek their own paths in an open and tolerant manner, without trying to impose their paths on others.

Many people, including some Christians, hold pluralistic views. Although they are spiritually dead and have been blinded by Satan (2 Corinthians 4:4), deeply spiritual non-Christians who may not even know what pluralism is will fight hard for the privilege of being pluralistic. They want to create their own spirituality, to enjoy the perceived freedom of religious diversity in which all truths are equal and no one faith reigns supreme. "Our truth works for us," they say, "but might not work for you. See what works for you and pursue it."

In *A New Religious America*, author Diana Eck quotes from a letter President Clinton sent to Sikh communities of America: "We are grateful for the teachings of Guru Nanak, which celebrate the equality of all in the eyes of God. . . . Religious pluralism in our nation is bringing us together in new and powerful ways." Eck adds, "Our society becomes stronger as each group's religious freedom is exercised and as people like the Sikhs articulate principles like equality and freedom in their own voice and in their own key."

Richard Conway, in the April 2002 issue of *Freedom Watch*, writes:

There are some things that, in my opinion, should not be legislated. Specifically, I'm referring to beliefs or actions that one person or group would propose to be the correct way for everyone to believe or act. I'm not talking about our individual responsibility to adhere to the universal truths that relate to right and wrong, although here, too, there are many who would be happy to legislate morality. I'm speaking of all individual rights to develop opinions and act accordingly.

Well-known pollster George Barna summarizes the effects of pluralism in *The Index of Leading Spiritual Indicators:*

Increasingly, faith commitment is viewed as a hobby rather than as a necessity for personal wholeness. . . . Adults' mental portrait of success in life resembles an aerial view of Washington, D. C.; the city is circled by the Beltway, with a substantial number of feeder highways leading to the encircling road, which permits entry to the city. Any of the feeder roads will get you to your destination; the options are equivalent, the choice is personal and idiosyncratic. . . . Christian churches that promote absolutes and which refuse to change their rules, traditions, and theological interpretations to accommodate the times are sometimes characterized by outsiders as "rigid" or intolerant.

Barna also points out that six out of ten Americans (58 percent) contend that no single religious faith has "all the answers to life's questions and challenges." It's no wonder that Christians who support biblical, "absolute truth" are perceived as being intolerant.

If there is no ultimate basis for determining truth, people argue, who is to judge what's true amidst the variety of truths? That's a good point. "Truth" becomes merely the current beliefs and values that are perceived to enable a social group to function well. Based on their perspectives, many non-Christians are right in saying that all truth is relative (but they may hate to admit that when they really understand relativism's implications). If the Bible isn't God's objective truth provided to humankind, as we believe, then non-Christians are correct in believing that we each must create our own truth or accept some or all of someone else's truth until better truth comes along.

If we are to communicate effectively with people holding this perspective, we must recognize that as the cultural view of religious truth changes, people's view of God changes. Consider the conclusions of Diana Eck: "We cannot live in a world in which our economies and markets are global . . . and yet live . . . with ideas of God that are essentially provincial, imagining that somehow the one we call God has been primarily concerned with us and our tribe. . . . The old-time religion has to be up to the challenges of an intricately interdependent world." In one sense she is quite right. Think of how many Christian denominations have fought over "tribal" issues. Churches have split over "tribal" issues. Non-Christians watch from the sidelines as Christians talk and even battle about how much God is blessing whom. I'm saddened and repelled by it, just as some of my non-Christians friends are.

In their search for "spirituality," many people are turning to the New Age movement. You can see this readily in the wide array of products displayed in the Spirituality or Religion section of any mainstream bookstore. A few years ago I entered a store that carried Christian gifts as well as tarot cards and spiritism books. It was apparent that the owner wanted to satisfy a wide range of customers.

The January 12, 2002, Colorado Springs *Gazette* featured an article urging parents to explore new religions with their children. Aminah, who raised her son Muslim, said that he had been exploring other religions since he was sixteen. (He was twenty-one when the article was published.) As writer Michelle Melendez notes, "She wants her son to find his own path to God, one that feels right to him."

Is it any wonder that many people today are skeptical about the existence of ultimate truth and choose to embrace pluralism? Doubt regarding ultimate truth has been prevalent for thousands of years. Helmut Thielicke, a German theologian and philosopher, writes in his book *Nihilism:*

Has not almost everybody who is sixty years old switched "isms" and thus changed the essential foundations of his life about three times during his lifetime? And have not the twenty-year-olds been quick to see this and developed a skepticism that clouds their youthful brows and has already imparted to their faces something that is not to be found in the youthful portraits of earlier generations . . . ? I would think that we might learn from association with the younger generation that they regard any proclamation of an absolute, whether it be by political parties or the forces of tradition—including Christianity—with a skepticism that filters out any such claim even before one approaches them at all.

PLURALISTIC TENSIONS

The lie that there is no right or wrong because there is no ultimate truth by which to judge people's actions resurged with force in the 1960s and 1970s and remains popular today. "Do what you want to do and be happy" was well received by people who wanted freedom without restraint. But those same people had a difficult time living with the consequences. It became apparent that there *is* right and wrong, or at least that certain things are quite harmful whether or not we believe that. The guy with the flower-painted VW bus wasn't happy when someone stole it. The man having sexual relations with his girlfriend felt hurt when she left him for another guy who was more fun. The drugs that felt good at

---

START A BOOK CLUB

Invite one or two Christian friends to join with you in holding a book club for neighbors and friends one evening a month. Participants can take turns choosing books the group will read, and one book can be discussed during each meeting. This provides a great forum for Christians and non-Christians to discuss topics of interest in a small, nonthreatening group.

first became enslaving and led to the deaths of many, including Janis Joplin and John Belushi.

During the 1960s and 1970s the writings of Friederich Nietzsche, the German philosopher who died in 1900, were popular among students and adults in the United States. Nietzsche preached that God is dead, and many people believed him. The only problem was, the consequences of being without God proved terrifying for those who understood the implications. Many people, including me, became agnostics instead of rejecting God's existence altogether, because it was far easier to say "I don't know" than to live with the consequences of atheism.

Since the beginning of humankind, people have railed against the firm boundaries of God's truth yet have had a difficult time living with the consequences of their rebellion. I have met a number of people who have broken God's laws while pursuing their own spiritual paths and have come to recognize the damaging consequences of their actions on themselves and others.

Today many non-Christians want the freedom of pluralism but find themselves caught in the tensions caused by failure to acknowledge and obey God's clear, universal truth found in the Bible. Their attempts to create personal standards of right and wrong, for example, yield many challenges for them—especially when they try to live in harmony with people who pursue different personal standards and live out different truths. As Brian McLaren points out, "If all religions are equally true, as pluralism claims, then each religion is false when it claims that some or all other religions are not true . . . which proves that pluralism (which claims that all religions are equally true) is false when it claims that all religions are true."

WHY THE BIBLICAL VIEW OF TRUTH MATTERS
Early one morning, soldiers dragged an influential man in his thirties before a tribunal in a Middle Eastern country. On trial for his life, he stood quietly as the judge listened to prosecutors' arguments. After hearing the arguments, the judge entered his chambers, summoned the prisoner and began questioning him privately.

The prisoner then had the audacity to state, "Everyone on the side of truth listens to me."

"What is truth?" the judge replied cynically and then paved the way for the prisoner's execution.

The judge was Pontius Pilate, Roman governor of Judea. The prisoner was Jesus Christ (see John 18:28-38).

Jesus knew truth because he was Truth embodied in the flesh (John 14:6). As God's Son, he knew that the Scriptures given through the Holy Spirit's anointing are God's transcendent words for humankind. They will forever be God's truth for us and all of reality.

Remember the discussion between Rachel and Carol at the beginning of this chapter? If the answers Rachel gives in defense of Jesus Christ are based only on her experiences and feelings, what she says can be easily discounted as opinion. That's why it's not enough for us only to communicate our personal stories of what God has done and is doing in our lives. We must also communicate the truth of Scripture to people who do not believe that there is God-given, universal truth that applies to all of reality. If we are to communicate this, it's essential that we have, and build, genuine respect and admiration for God's Word—God's *objective* truth—even though many people around us consider "objective truth" to be only opinion.

God's truth is not provincial, parochial or partial; it is universal in scope and application. Yet it allows for unique cultural expression and the creative individuality of people made in the divine image and redeemed through the Lamb. The truth does not flatten us out into faceless conformity, but liberates each of us to be who we ought to be under the Lordship of Christ.

DOUGLAS GROOTHUIS

Christianity is not based on personal experiences, even though a growing number of Christians believe this to be true. Christianity encompasses much more than what we think or feel about it, much more than the experiences we've had with God and how we feel about him.

Christianity is rooted in historical fact—including Jesus' life, death and resurrection—and God's ability to communicate his truth to us, whom he created. Unless we understand this, we risk communicating much less than we could and should of the essentials of biblical Christianity.

Unfortunately, the prevailing cultural views of truth are rapidly finding favor even among Christians. Fewer and fewer Christians value the Bible for what it is—God's transcendent, revealed, inspired truth given to his created people. When asked, most Christians will probably agree that God did inspire the writing of the Bible, but they may hesitate to emphasize such important doctrines as Jesus' being the only true way to God. In a national survey released in 2002 by Barna Research Online, only 32 percent of born-again Christians said they believed in moral absolutes.

As I began writing this chapter, I discussed its key points with Kerri, who became a Christian as an adult. She listened, then hesitantly said, "I'm not sure I believe what you believe. I know that Jesus is right for me, but I don't feel comfortable telling people he is the only way. Who knows if he is the only way?"

Kerri is not unique. Other people who claim to be Christians do not believe that the Bible is divinely inspired and inerrant. They say things like these:

- "I love the part about caring for needy people, but I don't like the verse that says Jesus is the only way to God. Many people find different spiritual truth that works for them."

- "I know the Bible says homosexuality is sinful, but I don't think it is. It's not their fault they are attracted to the same sex."

- "Satan doesn't really exist. He's just a symbol for evil."

- "I like verses that emphasize honesty, but why should I forgive my enemies?"

- "I know the Bible says I'm not to marry a non-Christian, but I love this guy and he loves me."

- "I'm all for the Judeo-Christian worldview—and other worldviews that work."

CHOOSING TO RESPOND WELL

How do we respond to pluralism? First, we have to recognize that it has permeated virtually every aspect of culture and that the biblical worldview is being challenged by other worldviews that promise to answer people's sincere questions. Then we must examine our hearts and minds, taking an honest look at what *we* believe concerning the Bible. Only when we affirm that the Bible is God's truth for us and all of reality can we confront pluralism—explaining what its real consequences are, revealing its deceitful core, showing its devastating effects, but doing so in love. Then we can speak of the Bible with joy and excitement.

In *The Bible Jesus Read*, Philip Yancey writes this concerning the

---

LOAN A BOOK

Sharing food for the stomach is one thing. Have you considered sharing food for the mind? Do you have a book that one of your neighbors might enjoy reading? It's easy to loan out books, particularly as you learn your neighbors' interests. One couple used our house-framing book to build a large workshop for their welding business. Another neighbor read our books to learn more about certain issues she was struggling with. A teenager (now grown) used to borrow Christian books from us regularly. I recently loaned a video curriculum on the Old Testament to a woman who is reading the Old Testament for the first time.

Bible: "By using a variety of authors and cultural situations, God developed a complete record of what he wants us to know; amazingly, the parts fit together in such a way that a single story does emerge." Scripture is an unfolding story, comprising many parts written in different styles over time, recording for created human beings God's fully inspired truth.

The Bible is the story of creation, sinful disobedience, judgment and forgiveness. It reveals God's unchanging character and commitment to his people. It is an unfolding story of God's love, reaching its climax in Jesus' coming to earth as a man to save sinners (1 Timothy 1:15), dying on the cross and bearing the sins of humanity on himself (Isaiah 53:6), and giving us a way to God through himself (Romans 1:16; 2 Corinthians 5:21; 1 Timothy 2:3-6).

The Bible is the story of salvation. All people are born sinful (Romans 3:23; James 2:10), and our sin separates us from God, who is holy. Without the blood of Christ that was shed for us on the cross (1 Peter 1:18-19; 1 John 2:1-2), we'd have no way to receive forgiveness and would suffer the penalty of eternal death (Romans 5:12; 6:23). But as 1 John 1:9 reveals, God will forgive our sins if we confess them to him. Jesus Christ died on the cross and rose again so that we could receive salvation through him and have a personal, dynamic, ongoing relationship with God.

The Bible shows how we are born again through Jesus and become a new creation (1 Corinthians 15:22; 2 Corinthians 5:17). Our old self has been crucified with Christ (Romans 6:6). We receive the free gift of eternal life (John 5:24; Romans 6:23).

The Bible is a story of triumph—Jesus' being raised from the dead (John 20), God's accomplishing his work on earth through frail human beings, and our certainty of spending eternal life with God (Titus 3:7).

The Bible records story after story of people who pursued God's truths faithfully and of people who refused to acknowledge him at all.

The Bible contains the laws by which we can prosper and which if ignored lead to spiritual death. It provides absolute standards of right and wrong, which apply and remain true whether or not we believe them.

It's time we let others know what the Bible really is and show them its relevance through sensitive discussion and godly love. The Bible is truly *the power of God!* "All Scripture is God-breathed and is useful for teaching, rebuking, correcting and training in righteousness" (2 Timothy 3:16). It is "living and active. Sharper than any double-edged sword, it penetrates even to dividing soul and spirit, joints and marrow; it judges the thoughts and attitudes of the heart" (Hebrews 4:12). The Bible is essential—in our lives, in touching the hearts and minds of non-Christians. Working through the Bible, the Holy Spirit challenges our mind, cultivates growth, convicts us of sin, heals our emotions and guides us down right paths.

"The Bible is our authority," writes Jim Petersen. "It is able to stand on its own against the unbeliever. Our job, as a witness, is not to defend it, but to give it an opportunity to work."

WHERE DO WE GO FROM HERE?

To build healthy relationships with those who don't know Christ personally, we need to actively seek to understand their beliefs and values, even when they are significantly different from ours. We have the responsibility to engage people where they are. We should strive to promote religious, racial and cultural harmony, but not harmony at all costs. Harmony does not mean that we should treat everybody's view of religious truth as God's truth. We are called to be respectful of different people and their spiritual beliefs, but fundamentally the Bible is not just another good book; it speaks firmly against the growing consensus that there is no universal truth from God and that there are many forms of the "divine."

We need to recognize and act on the Bible's unique claims to truth, personified in Jesus. We need to be convinced that the Bible is truth and that the only way to God is through Jesus. We need to spend time in the Bible, soaking up God's living truth. Only then we can effectively and enthusiastically share the truth of God's living Word with other people.

OUR GOD-GIVEN ROLE AND AUTHORITY

God has given us authority to be his representatives—his ambassadors—on earth. As God changes us from the inside out by his Spirit, he calls us to make his appeal known to people around us. Not only that, he empowers us to do it, knowing that not everyone will gladly receive what we have to share. "In this world you will have trouble," Jesus states. "But take heart! I have overcome the world" (John 16:33).

Through God's power, we can tell what God has done in our lives and introduce other people to the Bible's truths. We know the truth, and that

UNITE IN A COMMON CAUSE

Several years ago, a military training school began flying noisy, low-flying airplanes over a residential neighborhood and an elementary school in our area. People in our community banded together to get that situation resolved satisfactorily. It took several years, many meetings and numerous interviews on television. When things finally got worked out, my wife and I had made lasting friendships with non-Christians who had labored side by side with us.

truth has set us free (John 8:32). Our message of truth is backed by God's character, by the promises he makes in his Word and by his actions throughout eternity. His truth stands up to the most rigorous intellectual scrutiny and fulfills people's deepest needs.

Because the disciples knew in whom they believed and recognized the authority Jesus had given them, the disciples—doubting, fearful and impatient though they were—became bold. They stepped out in faith to proclaim the glorious truth, and the living God who had supernaturally given it. And God used them to literally turn the pagan world upside down. Today he wants to do the same thing through us!

We communicate the truth of God through who we are and the way in which we build relationships. We must strive to understand what non-Christians believe, why they believe it, and how God may want to use us to further what he is doing in their lives. And as we'll explore in the next chapter, we need to respond to their beliefs gently, without pressure.

FOR REFLECTION AND DISCUSSION

1. Why do you think many truth-seeking people don't consider the Bible to be authoritative, relevant and God-inspired?

2. How should we respond to people who claim to have found spiritual truth in something other than Jesus and the Bible? Why?

3. Do you find it easy or difficult to discuss the beliefs of non-Christians with them? Why?

4. How do we express God's love during discussions with non-Christians concerning truth?

5. People have said that in order to reach non-Christians' minds, we first must reach their hearts. Do you agree or disagree with this? Why? What's the relationship between our "wise and persuasive words" and the demonstration of the Holy Spirit's power working in and through us?

6. What steps can we take, from the very beginning, to ensure that discussions about spirituality don't cause rifts between us and non-Christians? How can we help to build mutual trust?

7. If we view our role as that of coming alongside what God is already doing in non-Christians' lives, how will we respond differently than we would if we believed everything (including their salvation) depended on what we say and do?

8. What effect(s) is pluralism having in your church? In your town or city? What, practically speaking, will it look like for you to challenge pluralistic thinking with your mind and heart seasoned with God's love and truth?

9. How can we communicate that we really do want to listen to and learn from non-Christians—to try to understand what it's like to walk in their shoes—while at the same time holding fast to the truth revealed in Jesus and the Bible?

10. What happens when Christians fail to seek to understand the beliefs and values of other people? What might the long-term effects be?

Offering Truth Without Pressure

"Gimme some space," is the cry of Unchurched Harry and Mary.

As Christians, many times we want to shower them with love and acceptance

and to enthusiastically tug them down the spiritual path toward Christ.

But most of them respond best when we back off enough to provide them with a place

where they feel safe to explore what it means to follow Jesus.

LEE STROBEL

Carrie, a Jewish woman, was in her apartment when someone knocked on her door. Upon opening it, she was confronted by a woman who literally threw a tract at her, burst into tears, shouted, "You are going to hell if you don't accept Jesus," and ran away down the hall.

A Christian woman who reached out to Carrie in college told me this story and how hostile it had made Carrie toward Christianity. Although it's an extreme example, her story illustrates why a number of non-Christians have been driven away from Christ and have such negative stereotypes of Christians.

As Lee Strobel says, non-Christians need space to explore Jesus' claims. We have the tendency to pile information on people while showing too little love. We listen too little and speak too often. We invite non-Christians to attend our churches but spend little time understanding their needs, longings, hopes, dreams and pain. And every time a non-Christian has a less-than-satisfactory encounter with someone who claims to be a Christian, the emotional and intellectual walls get higher.

A friend recently told me how he had zealously tried to convert his family after he became a Christian. The result? In a short time, he successfully alienated these loving family members, who years earlier had rescued him from a terribly dysfunctional home and virtually adopted him. Today he is working hard to rebuild those relationships, but it will take years to repair the damage he did in a few months.

I've discovered that many people who battle hard against Christianity have a terrible taste in their mouths from previous encounters with Christians. A nationally recognized photographer told me, "I used to trust people who call themselves Christians. But I soon learned that they are the last people to pay me for my services, and some never do."

Before they moved out of state, a married couple involved in a discussion group with my wife and me for more than two years repeatedly told us how much they disliked Christians who "had all the truth" and felt compelled to impose it on everybody else. They were tired of people looking down on them for being agnostics, tired of Christians preaching one thing and doing another. In response, they dedicated considerable energy to challenging Christians and Christianity as a whole.

What a sad commentary.

I know such situations happen because they also happened to me. As I evaluated the claims of Christ and the Bible, trying to figure out if Christianity was credible, Christians said many insensitive and unkind things to me. Some pressured me to stop seeking answers, to forget the ache I had inside because of the hypocrisy I'd seen, the easy answers I'd been urged to accept and my deep, unfulfilled longing for peace, hope and joy.

Finally I traveled to L'Abri in Switzerland, hoping to find a place where people would listen to me, provide answers to my serious questions, help me to overcome emotional issues I didn't fully understand,

and love me rather than judge me. I wasn't disappointed: my time at
L'Abri was life-changing.

Now my heart goes out to people who struggle with Christianity. I remember what it was like to be on the outside looking in but unwilling
to compromise intellectual integrity for what I then considered to be
"cheap faith." I realize why it can take many years for someone to turn
to Jesus—and why some never do—because it took me years. I know
that emotional barriers often feed intellectual barriers, because until
Christians helped me address my emotional needs I couldn't let down
my intellectual barriers. I cringe when I see Christians using high-

BUILD A HOUSE

Al, a friend of mine, got tired of talking about helping people
and wanted to *do it.* So he volunteered to work with Habitat for
Humanity in building a house for a needy family. A few weeks
ago he told me how amazed he has been at the number of discussions he has had with non-Christian volunteers at the job site.

pressure techniques on people who need genuine love and time to sift
through intellectual and emotional issues and barriers.

Part of our problem is that we have tended to use high-pressure evangelistic techniques more often than other ways of relating. We seem to be
more comfortable delivering facts than delivering loving relationship over
time. Perhaps it's because we don't think we have enough time to build
genuine relationships. Or we simply don't make building such relationships a high priority. Obviously it's much easier to give someone a quick
spiel or distribute Christian literature to people we don't know than to
help someone work through challenging spiritual issues week after week.

A Christian leader I met several years ago became a Christian in his
late twenties and, in his words, became "the most aggressive, hardcore,
competitive evangelist you could imagine." Believing evangelism was

knowledge based, he memorized Bible verses to counter objections and sought to "win" people for Christ. After arguing with non-Christians, he'd ask himself, *Did I win or lose?* During a year of depression, however, he reevaluated everything he had been taught about God and the Bible. He emerged with an entirely different understanding of God and began to lovingly share biblical truth in a context of relationship.

Certainly God can use all types and styles of evangelism: tracts, radio testimonials, television preaching, crusades, door-to-door visitation, one-on-one sharing in the street, serving others in practical ways, writing prophecy-related novels, engaging in intellectual debates with students the way the late Francis Schaeffer did. The real issue is how and why we approach people and the attitudes behind our actions.

The people who influence us most are not those who buttonhole us and talk to us, but those who live their lives like the stars in heaven and the lilies of the field, perfectly simply and unaffectedly. Those are the lives that mould us. If you want to be of use to God, get rightly related to Jesus Christ and He will make you of use unconsciously every minute you live.

OSWALD CHAMBERS

Do we approach people sensitively, honoring who they are and their needs and interests? Do we approach them out of love or with selfish, ulterior motives? Are we in touch with the Holy Spirit's leading or simply manufacturing opportunities in our own strength? Compare pressured, manipulative and insensitive approaches to sharing the gospel with the approach taught by the apostle Paul:

The Lord's servant must not quarrel; instead, he must be kind to everyone, able to teach, not resentful. Those who oppose him he must gently instruct, in the hope that God will grant them repentance leading them to a knowledge of the truth, and that they will come to their senses and escape from the trap of the devil, who has taken them captive to do his will. (2 Timothy 2:24-26)

MAKE MUSIC

Music, it's said, crosses all kinds of relational and cultural boundaries. And playing an instrument opens doors to plenty of discussions with other musicians. I have been playing harmonica for
more than thirty years now and have played with various musicians. Often discussions about music have led to discussions of
spiritual things.

Last year a friend and I played a small concert in our community.
We selected Christian songs that would communicate the gospel without being offensive to non-Christians, who made up most
of the audience.

Consider the time when Jesus, after healing hundreds of people in
Galilee, said, "Okay, people, it's time to believe in me. Unless you believe
now, before you start your cooking fires, I'm withdrawing my invitation
to give you salvation. By the way, if you receive me as Savior and Lord
within the next five minutes, I'll give each of you a coupon to a fish fry
and throw in one hundred loaves of bread miraculously made of organ-
ically grown, hand-ground wheat flour."

Does this sound right? Of course not. Jesus never said anything like
this. Yes, he urged people to come to him. Yes, he presented the gospel
in various ways. Yes, he emphasized the importance of repentance and
salvation and the dire consequences of not believing in him. But he
never pressured people. He never manipulated. Their choice remained
their choice.

Jesus knows, better than anybody who has ever lived, what is at stake
eternally. If anyone ever wanted people to choose him and receive eternal life, it is Jesus. When he came to earth, he was willing to, and did,
make huge sacrifices—including the utmost sacrifice of his life—so that
people could believe in him and escape the fires of hell. "For God did
not send his Son into the world to condemn the world, but to save the
world through him. Whoever believes in him is not condemned, but

whoever does not believe stands condemned already because he has not believed in the name of God's one and only Son" (John 3:17-18).

Jesus knew Lucifer well and all the details of hell. In fact, he said, "I saw Satan fall like lightning from heaven" (Luke 10:18). Yet as Jesus' interaction with a young man in Matthew 19 highlights, he still refused to pressure anyone to believe in him. We read that the guy walked up to Jesus and asked, "Teacher, what good thing must I do to get eternal life?" Clearly he believed that Jesus was different from other teachers, or he wouldn't have asked this question. He listened to Jesus' answer and asked two more questions.

As the conversation progresses, we can almost hear the guy getting more excited and thinking, *I haven't murdered, committed adultery, stolen or given false testimony. I have honored my father and mother. Hey, I have loved my neighbor as myself. I can do this!*

Then the verbal bomb drops. Jesus invites him to give up what has consumed the biggest place in his heart and mind—his material treasure. "If

FORM A NEIGHBORHOOD PLAY GROUP

If you have small children at home, talk with your neighbors about forming a play group. The parents and children can get together during designated times at one another's homes or in a park. If all goes well, the children will have fun with their peers, and you'll have a great time visiting and relaxing with new friends.

If you like kids and want to meet their parents, a play area may be just the ticket. One man in Ohio set up playground equipment in his backyard for his kids. Before long it became the rallying point for the entire neighborhood. Kids sniff out tire swings and other fun pieces of play equipment, and their parents are sure to follow. My wife and I have built several swings, and we are toying with the idea of building a "zip line" on which children can ride a long cable down one of our hills.

you want to be perfect," Jesus says, "go, sell your possessions and give to the poor, and you will have treasure in heaven. Then come, follow me."

We don't know what this man owned, but we can guess: a palatial home with running water, a set of racing camels with leather saddles, a closet full of tunics, plenty of gold and silver coins, attentive servants . . . After hearing Jesus' invitation, the man "went away sad, because he had great wealth." Having weighed the options, he decided to trust in his possessions. Did he ever decide to follow Jesus? Scripture doesn't tell us.

The way in which Jesus responded to the young man's decision is important. Jesus didn't run after him and beg him to receive the good news. Nor did he spew out apologetics to try to convince the young man. Even knowing what he knew of hell, Jesus honored the young man's choice (see Matthew 19:16-24). And I'm sure Jesus didn't walk away feeling like a failure because the young man didn't say *yes*, which is how some of us feel when people don't receive the gospel message when we first present it.

It's easy to shake our heads at this young man and think, *Why'd you walk away?* We give him low marks on the "how-did-he-respond-to-Jesus" quiz. But I think this guy deserves a little praise. At least he evaluated the options and made a sincere choice. He didn't weasel around. He didn't sell his camels to his brother-in-law for a token amount and plan to buy them back as soon as Jesus wasn't looking. He didn't transfer the title of his house to his cousin with the stipulation that it would revert to him in six months. No, he evaluated Jesus' offer and decided against it— at least right then. Maybe he reached a different conclusion later.

Many people today buy things impulsively, but deciding whether or not to trust in Jesus as Lord and Savior is not a decision to be made on the spur of the moment. We need to give non-Christians the opportunity to reflect on the gospel and the Christian faith. We need to help them work through their questions about God and the Bible—and anything else (including emotional issues) that keeps them from choosing a personal relationship with God through Jesus. Instead we often expect people to make immediate decisions for Christ. We expect them to make life-changing commitments to the Savior faster than they might choose to buy a washing machine, a car or a box of breakfast cereal on one of the high shelves in the grocery store.

How do you feel when a salesperson pressures you? Chances are you don't like it. That's why 735,000 people signed up on the U.S. do-not-call telemarketing list the first day it went into operation, June 27, 2003. During some parts of that day, according to the Federal Trade Commission, the do-not-call webpage was visited a thousand times a second.

Imagine how non-Christians who hear about Jesus' love and biblical truth feel and respond when they are pressured to make an eternal decision that will affect every aspect of their lives as well as the lives of their families. How are their decisions affected by a suspicion that we will lose interest in them, be critical of them or keep pressuring them if they don't choose Jesus immediately? I've seen people who were pressured to become Christians turn away in bitterness, believing that all Christians have a judgmental, bigoted attitude toward anyone who believes differently. I've also come to understand more of what may be going through non-Christians' minds as they evaluate Christianity as a whole and Jesus' claims in particular.

- "I have been doing things I know aren't right—but I'm not ready to stop doing them."
- "I am afraid of what my family and friends may say." (Think about a Muslim from Saudi Arabia, for instance, who could be killed in his or her home country as a result of choosing Christ while studying in the United States.)
- "I've spent a long time getting to where I am, and I don't want to give it up now. I like my career and material possessions."
- "I'm doing fine. Why do I need God?"
- "I'm too busy and pressured to get spiritual right now."
- "I'm drawn to Jesus, but how does what he taught differ from what other religious leaders taught? And why is Jesus the only way to God?"

Patiently coming alongside someone who is evaluating Christianity is

JOIN A LOCAL ENVIRONMENTAL GROUP

When I was a teenager, I helped a group of people clean debris out of a section of a nearby river. The city government contributed a backhoe and dump trucks and paid dump fees. It's amazing how much dialogue took place.

This summer I volunteered to work at a community site that accepts tree branches and pine needles, which are then ground up into mulch that is given away. This program is helping people in our area reduce the danger of forest fires. For four hours I showed people where to unload their pickups and trailers and in a quiet way showed that I care about the community. I also made new friends.

not without risk. It can be time consuming, cost money and force us to think about uncomfortable issues. It may also take years before the person chooses Jesus—and some never choose him.

You may be thinking, *But during their evaluation period, people will not yet be Christians. If they die before they decide, they will go to hell.* That's true, but we're not in the eternal life insurance business—"buy this policy and you'll escape hell." Nor should we be in the "drag-them-into-the-kingdom" business. We are in the life-changing relationship business, lovingly guiding people toward a healing, *lasting* personal relationship with God through Jesus Christ. God does the work of drawing people to himself; we are simply (and importantly) his ambassadors, trying to support what he is already doing in people's lives. The process of discovering Jesus isn't always easy, neat and quick. In fact, statistics show that the older people are, the less likely they are to choose Jesus.

We want people to repent of their sins and receive Jesus, but not because they feel pressure from us. We must not encourage anyone to put his or her mind or heart on hold and make a rash decision for Christ. Rather, we are called to answer people's questions. Peter writes, "Always be prepared to give an answer to everyone who asks you to give the reason for the hope that you have. But do this with gentleness and respect" (1 Peter 3:15).

A "decision for Christ" that doesn't lead to a dynamic, living and growing relationship with God doesn't have much meaning. We want people to make decisions for Christ that will stand the test of time, because tests of their faith will surely come! I have wrestled with God about many things, including a job loss, the deaths of family members, questions about my faith, financial problems, sins I enjoy. Any of my friends who make a commitment to Christ will no doubt face similar struggles. If their faith is well grounded from the beginning, it's more likely that during hard times their roots will go deeper into God and his Word.

Each of us needs space in which to think about spiritual things, work through issues and perhaps choose new directions. Non-Christians also need time to sort out and test new ideas, evaluate experiences and wrestle with troubling issues. It's far better for a non-Christian to ask tough questions during a course of months or even years than to simply agree to the basic salvation message and then drift on to the next popular spiritual guru or religion. Several people I've guided to Jesus drifted away years later. Consequently I've come to recognize the value of follow-up discipleship that helps new Christians become rooted in their faith.

> *We have to make room for people to struggle because the stakes are so big.*
>
> *We should not be too pleased if someone comes to Christ with little struggle—it may mean this is simply a compliant person, and the same compliance that eases them into Christianity may also ease them toward the next thing that calls for their obedience.*
>
> EARL PALMER

FOR REFLECTION AND DISCUSSION

1. Why do you think Christians sometimes pressure people to become

Christians? Describe times when you have either seen or experienced this. What happened as a result?

2. If you were not a Christian, how would you like to be treated by Christians? Why?

3. Do you agree that how and why we approach people, and the attitudes behind our actions, are far more important than the types and styles of evangelism we use? Why or why not?

4. What's the value of backing off and giving people room to evaluate Christianity?

5. What does it mean, in practical terms, to "gently instruct" people who aren't yet Christians? How can we, who already "know the truth," do this with humility and love?

6. Describe your journey toward Jesus. Was it long or short, easy or complicated? In what ways did Christians help or hinder you during your spiritual journey?

— 8 —

Understanding the Journey to Belief

He [Jesus] is the gospel. He is our message.

Everything else we Christians believe and hold dear is an outworking of this one truth.

If we are to be effective among the people of this generation,

our own understanding of Christ—the implications of His identity,

His death and His resurrection—must be dynamic and growing.

JIM PETERSEN

I met Mateen through my parents, at the church they attend in Illinois. Later I had the pleasure of sharing a meal with him and his family in their home.

Mateen grew up in Saudi Arabia. His father, an oil company executive, always maintained an appearance of Islam for himself, but the family didn't practice the tenets of Islam and lived pretty secular lives. Mateen was considered Muslim, because according to Muslim law, the son of a Muslim is Muslim.

Around age thirteen, Mateen became hungry for truth, wanting to know what, if anything, was at the center of life. An American couple visiting Saudi Arabia got him interested in an Eastern religious viewpoint. They pointed him to a book written by an Indian guru who tried to build bridges between Eastern and Western thinking.

GOD'S LOVE EXPRESSED IN RELATIONSHIP

Mateen read the book and began taking correspondence courses in yoga through the guru's organization. Because the oil company's school operated only through ninth grade, Mateen enrolled at Phillips Exeter Academy in New Hampshire; there he took courses in religion and practiced meditation. He knew nothing of Christianity and considered himself to be very spiritual and good. Often he participated in discussions about spiritual values in the academy chapel.

Then he was introduced to the love of Jesus when he returned to Saudi Arabia for summer vacation. He told me:

> Christian friends invited me to come to their weekly meetings, where they discussed their growth in Christ. When I was there, though, the topic always changed to a defense of the existence of God. Although I could be virulently anti-Christian in the context of arguments, they continued to welcome me into their circle. I always peppered them with questions. I wasn't trying to play games. I was trying to see if they'd say something that was new to me and somehow change my thinking.
>
> I was saying, "Prove to me that God exists," wanting a blackboard proof—premise 1, premise 2, therefore . . . conclusion. They gently said, "Mateen, we know God exists because we know him." That answer went right over my head. I was thinking about knowing *about* God, not knowing God. They claimed that Jesus was the way to salvation and was God who had come in the flesh.

Gradually their gentle, consistent love broke through Mateen's shell. "Those Christian friends were one of the greatest evidences of the grace of God incarnated through his people. I loved being with them but didn't think it had anything to do with their being Christians. They had a cohesiveness I didn't share. *It's your thing,* I thought, *and I have my Eastern beliefs.*"

During his senior year, Mateen read Erich Fromm's *The Art of Loving,* which emphasized that real love is deeper than surface emotions and

INVITE PEOPLE TO A CHRISTMAS OR EASTER SERVICE

Invite non-Christian friends and/or family members to go to church with you at Christmas or Easter. (For many of them, it's the only time they'll attend church.) It will mean even more if you (or a family member) will be participating in the program. After the service, take them out for a meal. What's important is making them feel welcome and letting them see the church up close without feeling any pressure.

that it's important to love people from your heart to their heart—deep level to deep level. *That's wonderful,* Mateen thought. *That's the way life ought to be. I'm going to be a loving person like that.* He kept studying Hindu, Buddhist and Taoist texts.

The summer before he entered Stanford University, Mateen met an Indian who taught yoga in Saudi Arabia. He tutored Mateen in classical yoga, which is based on progression through an eightfold path into a state of enlightenment or nirvana.

A CONTINUING QUEST FOR SPIRITUAL TRUTH

During his freshman year, Mateen declared a philosophy major, principally because of his search to find answers. He pursued interests in Eastern philosophy and religion but also took core classes in the Western philosophical tradition. "My courses were deeply exciting because I felt I was engaging ideas central to life, reading people who were tackling subjects I thought ought to be tackled. I was like a sponge sopping things up and trying things out. One of my favorite things was to get involved in late-night bull sessions with other students and try out proofs for God's existence or steer discussion toward questions of ultimate reality."

Then an incident rocked Mateen's foundation.

I was riding my ten-speed to my dormitory at lunchtime. Lots of kids were around. Normally I rode up to the front steps, hopped off the bike, pulled it up the front steps, parked the bike and ran inside. But as I neared the building, I saw a fellow student—an outcast who was not liked—sitting on the front steps sobbing. If you wanted to be cool, you didn't spend time with him.

Mateen, I thought, *you should stop and help him.* Immediately a second thought came: *No way am I going to stop in front of all these people and help him.* Instead of jumping off my bike, I continued riding around the dorm to a side entrance. I didn't think much about it right then, but by that evening what I'd done haunted me. *Where is this love I'm supposed to have for people? It wasn't in my heart for that guy.*

A few days later, still troubled and embarrassed, Mateen told his girlfriend how he felt. She replied, "That's just human nature. Just try your best and go on. Don't worry about it." But Mateen couldn't shake the memory of his selfishness. He realized the evil in his heart and could no longer think of himself as being basically a good person.

The next summer, Mateen studied at an ashram on the outskirts of Bombay, India. He recalls:

That was a turning point for me. I looked as deeply at yoga and Eastern mysticism as anything I'd ever studied up to that point, and still had deep questions. My last day in the ashram, the guru asked if I had any questions for him. "Yes," I said. "I have a big question. Does God exist?"

"If it helps you in your path to believe in God, then believe," he said. "If it doesn't help, don't worry about it."

Either God exists or he doesn't, I thought. *If he does and I don't believe in him, that's a big mistake. If I do believe in him, and he exists, that's a great plus. If he doesn't exist but I do believe in him, I haven't lost anything.* So I pressed on: "Many of my friends claim that Jesus is God. What do you think of that?"

The guru answered, "Jesus, in a sense, is God, just like Buddha, Krishna, Muhammad and Confucius." I knew then that he believed Jesus to be what in Hindu philosophy is called an avatar, almost like an incarnation of the divine universal mind that occasionally bubbles up in history to provide divine guidance for human beings. So he was saying that Jesus was great but not unique. I knew from my Christian friends that Jesus made unique claims no one else could match, so I was also dissatisfied with this answer.

When Mateen left India at age nineteen, licensed to teach classical yoga, seeds of doubt had been planted. He thought, *Here's a man in his nineties from the Brahmin caste—the highest religious caste—who has been practicing classical yoga for most of his life—at least eighty years—and he doesn't have answers any more certain than mine. If I stay on this path, where am I going to get when I reach his age, if I get that old?*

CHALLENGED BY THE POWER OF LOVE

Back in Saudi Arabia the summer after his sophomore year, Mateen began dating Nancy, an American Christian whose family had just moved to Saudi Arabia. One day she said, "Mateen, we could never get too serious because you are not a Christian, and I could never think about marrying someone who is not a Christian. Jesus Christ is number one in my life, and whoever is number two also has to want Jesus to be number one in his life."

At that point Mateen became angry. *Why does she love someone more*

SET UP A NEIGHBORHOOD MINISTRY TO SINGLE MOTHERS

Have you learned a bit about rearing children? Understand the special needs of mothers? Maybe you could reach out in special ways to single mothers: providing advice and childcare, teaching financial principles and so on. Because families are spread out in our society, many single mothers do not have close family members in town. Begin with mothers in your local church or neighborhood.

than me? he thought. *I wouldn't put anybody in front of her. Why is she putting this Jesus in front of me?* "Well," he replied, "I guess we'll go our separate ways, because I can't just change my whole view of what's right and wrong for a relationship. There's not much integrity in that."

Nancy left to start school at Ouachita Baptist University in Arkansas in late August. After she'd been gone a week, Mateen decided he would like to visit her on his way to Stanford. Her dad, who had traveled to help her get settled at college, was scheduled to return to Saudi Arabia in a few days and had her phone number and address.

Mateen's flight left, however, before Nancy's father returned. Mateen stayed in London overnight, then went to the transit lounge in London's Heathrow Airport. There someone called his name. It was Nancy's father, waiting for his plane. He gave Mateen Nancy's phone number and address.

How convenient that was, a nice coincidence, he thought, little realizing how God was gently working out his plans.

Surprised by Mateen's call from the Little Rock Airport, Nancy and a friend picked him up, took him to the university and found a place for him to stay in a dormitory. Pleased to be near her, Mateen was also wary.

I knew this was a Christian place where Bible-thumpers would probably try to thump me. I didn't want that. I'd already been in arguments with Christians in Saudi Arabia. I knew the basics of the gospel message, but I didn't believe it and didn't want anybody to pressure me.

When Nancy was in classes and when we were together, I watched people. I kept seeing students my age treating one another with love and kindness, the way I knew human beings ought to treat one another. I remembered how I'd avoided being loving toward the guy on the Stanford campus and felt an emptiness in my heart. Because these students had something I didn't have, I began asking them where they got the power to love people like that. And they'd always say, "Jesus."

"I'm not interested in the religious stuff," I'd answer. "I just want to know where you get the power to love people like that."

THE BIBLE'S TRUTH PENETRATES THE HEART AND MIND

After a number of people told Mateen they loved because of Jesus, he asked a student, "Okay, how do I find out about Jesus?"

"Read the Gospels," the student replied.

"What are the Gospels?" Mateen asked.

"They are in the New Testament and tell the story of Jesus' life."

"Where do I find them?"

The student gave Mateen a Bible, opened it to the book of Matthew and said, "Start here, and read until you finish the book of John."

OUR INFLUENCE FOR CHRIST IS FAR GREATER THAN WE REALIZE

The next day I was sitting outside reading the Gospels and waiting for Nancy to get out of class. A guy wearing shorts and no shirt, with perspiration pouring off him, was pushing a lawnmower up and down a large field. Then about half a dozen kids came out of a dorm, walked past me and headed off in a car. They returned about fifteen minutes later, carrying food.

Suddenly one guy peeled off from the group and offered a huge soda to the guy who was mowing. They both were only twenty yards from me, so I could see that the guy mowing was stunned and thankful. Clearly he hadn't asked anybody to bring the drink. The other guy then went back into the dormitory.

As I saw that, I thought, *That was the right thing to do. That's the way a human being ought to think about another human being. Mateen, that would have been the furthest thing from your mind. You wouldn't even have seen that guy mowing.*

That incident, along with others he witnessed during his visit, made Mateen realize that human beings are actually capable of thinking unselfishly and loving others. But he knew that such love wasn't in his heart. These Christians kept talking about Jesus as the One who made it possible to have a heart like that. Seeing love in action in their lives made

START A BIBLE STUDY IN YOUR HOME

Friends of ours have been leading one for years now, and it has led to deep friendships with non-Christians. A number of books provide helpful tips on doing this, such as *Life-Style Evangelism* by Joseph Aldrich (Multnomah Press) and *Your Home a Lighthouse* by Bob and Betty Jacks (NavPress). Because of the nature of this kind of study, you might invite only people you know pretty well who are eager to learn more about the Bible. Also, be careful not to have hidden agendas. Give participants plenty of space to think about and explore the Bible passages, and encourage honest discussion.

Mateen willing to seriously evaluate the possibility that Jesus might be able to do something in his heart too.

I was twenty years old and for the first time was reading the Bible (other than the times I opened it to do proof-texting in philosophy classes). It took me three days to read through the four Gospels, and it was almost a surreal experience. I felt like I had plunged into the world of the New Testament and almost became oblivious to the twentieth-century world. I'd go with Nancy and her friends to a cafeteria to eat but wasn't interested in eating. My nose was planted in the Bible, and they were wise enough not to interrupt me.

At the end of three days, I came up for air and said to myself, *If there ever has been anyone worth giving your life to follow, it would have to be this man, Jesus.* For me that was a big statement to make. I'd had two years of philosophy at Stanford and been exposed to the lives and thoughts of many philosophers. I'd also seriously studied Hinduism, Buddhism, Taoism, Confucianism, Shintoism, Zoroastrianism, and of course Islam, plus the leaders of all those movements. I knew Christians believed that Jesus wasn't just a man, that he was God who'd come in the flesh, and I wasn't ready to agree to that. But I did say, "There's nothing more important to me than learning more about Jesus."

USING GOD-GIVEN OPPORTUNITIES WISELY

Mateen set up meetings with a New Testament professor, the dean of students and others. They listened patiently to his concerns and counter-claims. During these days, he felt as if a physical tug of war were going on inside his brain. His Eastern views still had a hold on him, yet he knew his belief system was bankrupt. So many "coincidences" seemed to confirm things people had told him about Jesus.

It's too painful to keep sitting on the fence, he thought. *I feel like I'm being pulled in both directions. I've got to take a step. If there weren't anything substantive about Jesus' claims and the reality of his presence in the lives of the people I'm looking at, I wouldn't be having this deep struggle.*

On September 15, Mateen asked Nancy how a person becomes a Christian. She replied, "You just pray."

"How does a person pray?" he responded.

"You talk to Jesus as if he's sitting right here next to us, and tell him what you want, how you are feeling. If you recognize that you need to be forgiven and rescued from the sins of your life, tell him that. Tell him you want him to be your Savior and Lord."

Mateen was silent for a little while, then said, "I'd like to do that."

"Okay," she replied, "I'll pray first, then you pray."

Remembering that moment, Mateen says, "A tremendous sense of release and relief flooded through me as I began praying. I felt great peace and great joy. I was no longer on the fence. I'd stepped over into the camp of Jesus, and he welcomed me."

Today Mateen pastors a vibrant church and gently guides other people into God's kingdom.

ORDINARY PEOPLE, AN EXTRAORDINARY CALLING

How might God want to use you today?

God may want to use you as he used those young students in Saudi

Arabia, who gave Mateen the opportunity to ask difficult questions about Jesus and demonstrated Jesus' love toward him and one another.

God may want to use you the way he used Nancy's father, to be a link between a searching non-Christian and a Christian.

God may want to use you as he used the professors, to answer a seeking person's intellectual questions honestly and compassionately.

God may want to use you to lead someone to Jesus, after other Christians have planted and watered the spiritual seeds.

When Jesus recruited his disciples, he selected remarkably ordinary people. He didn't do some of the obvious things he could have done when seeking candidates whom God would count on to fulfill an extraordinary calling on his behalf.

He didn't ask for résumés highlighting prospective candidates' accomplishments in fishing, using money, crowd control, public speaking, water walking or swordsmanship.

He didn't post help-wanted notices in marketplaces.

He didn't listen in on rabbis' teachings and recruit those who were well versed in religious laws and traditions.

He didn't inquire at the city gates or in synagogues to discover which people had the strongest political ties to the Roman administrators.

He didn't read current demographics scrolls and evaluate which candidates could help him reach targeted people groups most effectively.

He didn't find out which families listed in the *Who's Who of Jerusalem* could provide financial resources to someone serving in ministry.

No, Jesus selected ordinary people like you and me to represent him on earth, people whose hearts were drawn toward him. And he still depends on the same kind of people today to represent him well on earth.

People all around us are seeking what Jesus offers. God says to us, in effect: "Pray for people who need me. I want to give you what you need and so much more so that my love, grace and joy overflows from you to them. Come to me, all you who labor. I have the power and grace you need. I want to work through your weaknesses to touch others. Let me gently love them through you. I want you to feel the joy of seeing others

SPONSOR A GAME NIGHT IN THE PARK

Invite coworkers and/or neighbors you'd like to know better. Play volleyball, croquet, softball, Frisbee golf or capture-the-flag. Then have a potluck meal together. This is a great activity for singles and families and can accommodate people of all ages.

come to me, but don't worry about whether you sow, cultivate, plant or reap. Love me, love others, and let me unfold my plans for you and other people in my time frame. I don't ask you to be perfect; I ask you to be faithful—to simply trust and obey."

When you and I obediently walk with God, drawing from him and in turn giving out to others, we will make a difference in our world. Let's take the following words by Charles Spurgeon to heart:

> What are we sent into the world for? Is it not that we may keep men in mind of God, whom they are most anxious to forget? If we are imitators of God, as dear children, they will be compelled to recollect that there is a God, for they will see His character reflected in ours. I have heard of an atheist who said he could get over every argument except the example of his godly mother: he could never answer that. A genuinely holy Christian is a beam of God's glory and a testimony to the being and the goodness of God. . . . We ought not only to be reminders of the careless, but teachers of the ignorant by our walk and conversation. When they look us up and down, and see how we live, they ought to be learning somewhat of God. Holy men are the world's Bibles: those who read not the Testament, read our testimony.

FOR REFLECTION AND DISCUSSION

1. How did Mateen's Christian friends respond to his serious questions and skepticism? What attitude(s) did they express toward him?

2. Which people shared their lives, and not just words, with Mateen? Why do you think their love had such an impact on him?

3. What does Mateen's story reveal about the ways in which God uses people to cultivate the soil of someone's heart? To plant spiritual seeds? To water the seeds? To take part in the spiritual harvest?

4. What might have happened if Christians had condemned Mateen for exploring Eastern religions? If they had become impatient because he required so much time and effort? If they had not listened respectfully to his viewpoints and sought to find areas of common ground with him? If they had pressured him to make a decision for Jesus instead of leaving him room to struggle?

5. What does this story demonstrate about the importance of listening to a non-Christian, asking questions and finding out about his or her perspectives?

6. Why was it important for Christians to address the needs of Mateen's heart, not just issues of his mind? What do you think they learned from him?

7. What are some of the ways in which God clearly was working behind the scenes, guiding his people as he drew Mateen to himself? How intentional were Christians in connecting with him?

8. What does this story reveal about the importance of using the influence we have, rather than comparing ourselves to other people and thinking we are insignificant?

9 What did you find interesting about Mateen's search for truth?

10. Why was it important for Mateen to read the Gospels? Why did his reading have such an effect on him? What does this reveal about the power of God's Word to influence people's hearts and minds?

Epilogue

I hold in my hand a little brochure titled "Jane's Story." Jane was my mother, who died of cancer on the morning of December 3, 2001. The brochure is based on a talk she had given at her church several years earlier, and she had made it available so that people might know the difference Jesus made in her life and come to know him too.

I was with Mom during her final week as she shared smiles and coffee with my father, who would sit on the edge of her bed. I was also present when my father invited Mom's friends to be with her the Saturday before she died. They came in by ones and twos. Some were young, some were older, but each of their lives had become intertwined with Mom's life. As they sat next to her, they prayed prayers that focused on heavenly hope. They cried tears of sadness mixed with thankfulness for the ways in which my mother had impacted their lives. Sometimes Mom smiled; other times she seemed to be asleep yet could hear.

As I greeted those beloved Saturday visitors, I was reminded again of the cycle of life. We enter the world, live out our allotted days, then die. Our lives are like flowers that grow and then wither (James 1:10-11).

Although in light of eternity each of us is not on earth for very long, much happens within each of our lives. New thoughts. Struggles. Deep emotions. Decisions of character. Relationships that come and go. People we meet briefly. People we know for years. The love and truth we reflect to other people truly make a difference in our little corners of the world.

That Saturday I picked up an elderly woman who no longer drives and wanted to be with Mom one last time. As we talked, she said, "When your mother first had cancer many years ago, I brought your family a meal." Until that moment, I hadn't been aware that she had voluntarily reflected Jesus' light to me. When I drove that woman back to her home and walked her to the door, deep emotions filled me. I had no words to express my thankfulness for the ways in which her life had blessed my family during so many years. So I simply leaned down and kissed her forehead.

After my mother died, copies of "Jane's Story" were handed out at the funeral home when friends gathered to reminisce about her. But her story didn't end there, nor did it end after the memorial service the next day. The impact she made in others' lives continues to spread, like ripples on a pond after a child throws in a rock. The story she wrote about her life and discovery of Jesus has traveled, person to person, to hospice people throughout the area, through local churches and through family members.

Why do I share this? It reminds me of why I decided to write this book.

I believe that relationships—our relationship with God and our relationships with other people—are the most important things in our lives. And they are the only things that truly last after we leave this earth. No matter who we are or where we live, we have opportunities through our words and actions to make an eternal difference in the lives of people all around us, especially non-Christians.

Years ago I flew on an airplane with Mother Teresa in India. I was on one side of the aisle; she was on the other. As soon as the flight attendant brought our meals, I wolfed down my rolls. Then, hearing a crinkling sound, I turned my head. Mother Teresa was carefully wrapping up her rolls in a napkin.

Noticing my curious look, she smiled and said, "For the children. For the children."

What great opportunities we have to *tell* and *show* others how they can know Jesus—the Bread of Life—and receive living water! Will we let others know what he has done for us, and share the Bible's truth, during the time we have left? Will we let these words penetrate our hearts and minds?

> Now we know that if the earthly tent we live in is destroyed, we have a building from God, an eternal house in heaven. . . . Christ's love compels us, because we are convinced that one died for all, and therefore all died. And he died for all, that those who live should no longer live for themselves but for him who died for them and was raised again.
>
> So from now on we regard no one from a worldly point of view. . . . [God] has committed to us the message of reconciliation. We are therefore Christ's ambassadors, as though God were making his appeal through us. (2 Corinthians 5:1, 14-16, 19-20)

Appendix 1

How Well Do You Know Your Neighbors?

On a full-size sheet of paper, draw a rough map of your home or apartment and the five houses or apartments that are closest to it. In each square, fill in as much of the following information about your neighbors as you can. Then give yourself the number of points designated for each answer and add up your score.

1. Last name(s) of household (1 point each)

2. First name of each adult in household (1 point each)

3. First names of children (1 point each)

4. Occupation of each adult (2 points each)

5. Age or grade in school of each child (2 points each)

6. How long they have lived in current home (2 points)

7. State in which each adult grew up (3 points each)

8. A favorite activity for each adult and child (3 points each)

9. Religious beliefs of each adult (4 points each)

10. Something you admire about each adult or child (4 points each)

Bonus: Add 5 points for each home you have entered. Add 25 points for each household you have invited over for a meal.

Penalty: Subtract 5 points for each neighbor you would not recognize on sight.

YOUR SCORE

1-25   You've made a start, but you have a long way to go. Why
            not plan a neighborhood open house?

26-50   You know more than the basics, but it's time to learn more
            about your neighbors. Think about inviting a neighboring
            family or single to join you in an activity.

51-110   You're well on your way to forming relationships with
            your neighbors. Think of one way in which you could
            deepen a friendship you've started. Then do it this week.

111 and up Congratulations! You've worked hard at getting to know
            your neighbors and are beginning to reap the rewards.
            This week, let people who live nearby know how much
            you appreciate them.

Appendix 2

Leading and Promoting Group Discussion

The "For Reflection and Discussion" questions at the end of each chapter can be used individually or in a group. Points to keep in mind concerning the questions:

- They are designed to be jumping-off points. Feel free to add your own questions based on your knowledge of participants and their experiences.
- Don't feel as if you have to ask every question. Your group may choose to focus on several of them instead.
- If all the questions are not covered, you may suggest that participants answer them later on their own.

GENERAL GUIDELINES

1. Be sure you have read the chapter(s) that will be covered during the discussion and have taken notes as needed.
2. You may choose to combine chapters or focus on each one individually, depending on your group's time frame and interests.
3. Be aware that participants will have differences of opinion and also will have had different experiences relating to non-Christians.
4. Give participants the opportunity to participate at their own comfort levels. At first some may be hesitant to answer questions because they are uncomfortable talking in a group.

5. Don't worry if participants are silent sometimes after you ask a question. If people truly are unable or unwilling to respond, respond to the question yourself and then invite others to do the same.

6. As you ask questions, be sure to listen to each individual's response. The process of thinking through issues is much more important than specific answers.

7. Interact with the questions. Reword them if necessary. Create new ones.

8. If you want to expand the discussion, pull out some quotations from each chapter and build questions around them. The quotes highlighted in each chapter may be good ones to use.

9. If someone starts to monopolize discussion, direct questions to other participants. If need be, talk to the person afterward and emphasize why it's important for everyone to have the freedom to participate.

10. If a heated theological debate erupts, encourage those involved to continue their discussion with you later, after the group time is over.

11. Encourage participants to share with you, before or after each discussion session, what they are thinking, learning and feeling. This will give you opportunities to connect with them individually and help you to guide the sessions more effectively.

12. Enjoy this time. The points you are helping to bring out may be life-changing for both the participants and the non-Christians they will reach with Jesus' truth and love!

13. Last, but not least, pray for the group and ask other people to pray too. Ask God for wisdom in leading the group and in using this material to accomplish great things in your lives.

Sources

Chapter 1

Linda Raney Wright, *Christianity's Crisis in Evangelism* (Gresham, Ore.: Vision House, 1995), p. 21.

Callout

Rich Nathan, *Who Is My Enemy?* (Grand Rapids: Zondervan, 2002), p. 25.

Chapter 2

Charles Colson and Nancy Pearcey, *How Now Shall We Live?* (Wheaton, Ill.: Tyndale House, 1999), p. 379.

Callouts

Dwight L. Moody, *The Overcoming Life* (Chicago: Moody Press, 1995), pp. 66-67.

John R. W. Stott, *Who Is My Neighbor?* (Leicester, U.K.: Inter-Varsity Press, 1995), p. 24.

Rebecca Manley Pippert, *Out of the Saltshaker & into the World,* rev. ed. (Downers Grove, Ill.: InterVarsity Press, 1999), p. 62.

Rich Nathan, *Who Is My Enemy?* (Grand Rapids: Zondervan, 2002), p. 34.

Chapter 3

Dick Staub, *Too Christian, Too Pagan* (Grand Rapids: Zondervan, 2000), p. 90.

Callout

David W. Henderson, *Culture Shift* (Grand Rapids: Baker, 1998), p. 41.

Chapter 4

Roger Steer, *Spiritual Secrets of George Müller* (Wheaton, Ill.: Harold Shaw, 1985), pp. 110-11.

Dwight L. Moody, *The Overcoming Life* (Chicago: Moody Press, 1995), pp. 62-63, 67.

Callouts

Lee Strobel, *Inside the Mind of Unchurched Harry & Mary* (Grand Rapids: Zondervan, 1993), pp. 89-90.

Chapter 5

Charles Colson and Nancy Pearcey, *How Now Shall We Live?* (Wheaton, Ill.: Tyndale House, 1999), pp. 33-34.

Bill Hybels, "Speaking to the Secular Mind," in *Growing Your Church Through Evangelism and Outreach,* ed. Marshall Shelley (Nashville: Moorings, 1996), p. 109.

Callouts

Peter Deison, *The Priority of Knowing God* (Grand Rapids: Discovery House, 1990; Grand Rapids: Kregel, 2000), p. 26.

Howard Hendricks, *Standing Together* (Gresham, Ore.: Vision House, 1995), p. 11.

Chapter 6

Os Guinness and John Seel, eds., *No God but God* (Chicago: Moody Press, 1992), p. 213.

David Brooks, *Bobos in Paradise* (New York: Simon & Schuster, 2000), pp. 234-35.

Diana Eck, *A New Religious America: How a "Christian Country" Has Now Become the World's Most Religiously Diverse Nation* (San Francisco: HarperSanFrancisco, 2001), p. 7.

Richard Conway, "My Flag's Bigger Than Your Flag," *Freedom Watch*, April 2002, p. 3.

George Barna, *The Index of Leading Spiritual Indicators* (Dallas: Word, 1996), pp. 6, 15.

Ibid., p. 14.

Eck, *New Religious America*, p. 24.

Michelle Melendez, "Parents, Kids Should Explore New Religions Together," *Colorado Springs Gazette,* 12 January 2002, Life section, p. 5.

Helmut Thielicke, *Nihilism,* trans. John W. Doberstein (1961; reprint, New York: Schocken, 1969), p. 22.

Brian McLaren, *Finding Faith* (Grand Rapids: Zondervan, 2000), pp. 148-49.

Barna Research Online, "Americans Are Most Likely to Base Truth on Feelings," February 12, 2002, <http://www.barna.org/FlexPage.aspx?Page=BarnaUpdate&BarnaUpdateID=106>.

Philip Yancey, *The Bible Jesus Read* (Grand Rapids: Zondervan, 1999), p. 21.

Jim Petersen, *Living Proof* (Colorado Springs: NavPress, 1989), p. 177.

Callouts

S. D. Gaede, *When Tolerance Is No Virtue* (Downers Grove, Ill.: InterVarsity Press, 1994), p. 59.

Douglas Groothuis, *Truth Decay* (Leicester, U.K.: Inter-Varsity Press, 2000), p. 73.

Chapter 7

Do-not-call telemarketing list: *Colorado Springs Gazette,* June 28, 2003, p. A1.

Callouts

Oswald Chambers, *My Utmost for His Highest* (New York: Dodd, Mead & Company, 1935), p. 139.

Earl Palmer, "Giving People Time and Space," in *Growing Your Church Through Evangelism and Outreach,* ed. Marshall Shelley (Nashville: Moorings, 1996), pp. 14-15.

Chapter 8

Charles Spurgeon, *Day by Day with C. H. Spurgeon,* comp. Al Bryant (Waco, Tex.: Word, 1980), pp. 215-16.

THE BOOK CLUB FOR TODAY'S CHRISTIAN FAMILY

A Letter to Our Readers

Dear Reader:

In order that we might better contribute to your reading enjoyment, we would appreciate your taking a few minutes to respond to the following questions. When completed, please return to the following:

Andrea Doering, Editor-in-Chief
Crossings Book Club
401 Franklin Avenue, Garden City, NY 11530

You can post your review online! Go to www.crossings.com and rate this book.

Title _____ Author _____

1 Did you enjoy reading this book?

❑ Very much. I would like to see more books by this author!

❑ I really liked_____

❑ Moderately. I would have enjoyed it more if_____

2 What influenced your decision to purchase this book? Check all that apply.

    ❑ Cover
    ❑ Title
    ❑ Publicity
    ❑ Catalog description
    ❑ Friends
    ❑ Enjoyed other books by this author
    ❑ Other _____

3 Please check your age range:

    ❑ Under 18   ❑ 18-24
    ❑ 25-34   ❑ 35-45
    ❑ 46-55   ❑ Over 55

4 How many hours per week do you read? _____

5 How would you rate this book, on a scale from 1 (poor) to 5 (superior)?

_____

Name_____

Occupation_____

Address_____

City_____ State_____ Zip_____